RU 486

BOOKS BY LAWRENCE LADER

1955
Margaret Sanger and the Fight for Birth Control

1961
The Bold Brahmins: New England's War
Against Slavery (1831–1863)

1966
Abortion

1969
Margaret Sanger: Pioneer of Birth Control
(with Milton Meltzer)

1971
Breeding Ourselves to Death

1972
Foolproof Birth Control: Male and Female
Sterilization

1973
Abortion II: Making the Revolution

1979
Power on the Left: American Radical Movements Since 1946

1987
Politics, Power, and the Church

RU 486

The Pill That Could End the Abortion Wars and Why American Women Don't Have It

LAWRENCE LADER

ADDISON-WESLEY PUBLISHING COMPANY, INC.
Reading, Massachusetts   Menlo Park, California
New York   Don Mills, Ontario   Wokingham, England
Amsterdam   Bonn   Sydney   Singapore   Tokyo
Madrid   San Juan

Many of the designations used by manufacturers and sellers to distinguish their products are claimed as trademarks. Where those designations appear in this book and Addison-Wesley was aware of a trademark claim, the designations have been printed in initial capital letters (e.g., Cytotec).

Library of Congress Cataloging-in-Publication Data

Lader, Lawrence.
    RU 486 : the pill that could end the abortion wars and why American women don't have it / Lawrence Lader.
        p.   cm.
    Includes index.
    ISBN 0-201-57069-6
    1. Mifepristone—Social aspects—United States.   2. Abortion—Social aspects—United States.   I. Title.
    RG137.6.M53L33   1991
    363.4'6—dc20   90-24451
                                                                          CIP

Copyright © 1991 by Lawrence Lader

Cover design by Mike Stromberg
Text design by Joyce C. Weston
Set in 10½-point Meridien by Maple-Vail, Binghamton, NY

1 2 3 4 5 6 7 8 9-MW-9594939291
First printing, February 1991

For our daughter, Wendy Summers Lader

Contents

Introduction

It is a peculiar phenomenon of American politics that the abortion conflict has become increasingly violent—the most divisive issue of our time—since the U.S. Supreme Court legalized abortion in 1973. Few Americans under age thirty-five remember the conflict's origins. Even fewer understand the impact of RU 486, the new French abortion pill, or even how we have reached this crisis, especially considering the fact that abortion was essentially legal in the early decades of this country's history.

Abortion, in fact, was hardly a subject of debate until the Civil War period. Under English common law, the basis of our colonial courts and the U.S. court system for many years, abortion at the early stage of pregnancy was never a crime. Two rulings by Massachusetts courts in 1812 and 1845 declared that abortion with the woman's consent was not punishable before "quickening," or approximately the time when the fetus moved in the womb. Nearly all the state courts handed down similar decisions in the early to mid-nineteenth century. Some states—Arkansas and Mississippi, for example—never criminalized abortion before quickening until the mid-twentieth century.

The development of prohibitive state laws on abortion shortly before the Civil War, and increasingly after 1865, had its roots in a number of causes. As part of the campaign to protect public health (England, as one example, made smallpox vaccination compulsory in 1853), the medical profession became determined to eliminate the damage and death often suffered by women at the hands of unlicensed practitioners of abortion. New Jersey's Supreme Court in 1858 expressed this philosophy by ruling that the state's new anti-abortion law had been passed "not to prevent the procuring of abortions so much as to guard the health and life of the mother against the consequences of such attempts."

The dogma of the Catholic church, defining the start of personhood from the moment of conception, had no influence in this period. Still basing its decision on the common law, the New York State Court of Appeals, the state's highest court, ruled in 1872 that "the child does not 'quicken', that is, become endowed with life" in early pregnancy.

A second motivation for these anti-abortion laws at a time when contraception hardly existed was the need to boost America's population. In the face of rampant disease and minimal health care, families of ten children were lucky if two lived to age twenty-one. New workers were critical to the nation's booming industry, and agricultural hands were in short supply in the vast Western farmlands. A Pennsylvania court, summarizing this viewpoint in 1850, labeled abortion a "flagrant crime because it interferes with and violates the mysteries of nature by which the human race is propagated and continued."

Finally, the Puritan obsession with sin, reaching its peak in the Victorian era, considered abortion a means through which unwed women could "avoid their Shame and escape punishment," as a New Hampshire law put it. The illegitimate child represented public proof of a woman's fall much as Hawthorne's "scarlet letter" represented the stamp of adultery. This form of female degradation permeated the medical profession. During the early experiments with anesthesia in childbirth, many doctors as well as portions of the public protested, arguing that it would be a sin to deprive women of the privilege of suffering. In fact, the medical profession promoted the thesis that a woman's body was its exclusive provenance, and that any attempts by women to control it, whether by abortion or contraception, should be eliminated. These beliefs culminated with the federal Comstock Law of 1873, which enabled Anthony Comstock, special agent for the New York Society for the Suppression of Vice, and his allies to wage open war on everything from pornography to abortion. Significantly, Madame Restell (born Caroline Trow), calling herself a "female physician," had practiced abortion without hindrance from her mansion at Fifth Avenue and Fifty-second Street since 1838, but Comstock had her arrested and closed her practice in 1878.

Although women had long depended upon abortion to regulate the birth of their offspring, at least since the practice was first recorded in the royal archives of China in 3000 B.C., by the 1890s, abortion had been made a crime in almost every state. From the late nineteenth century on, pregnant women had few options. They could try to end the pregnancy themselves, desperately resorting to such tools as knitting needles and coat hangers or the injection of powerful detergent solutions, which generally caused injury and often death. Watching lines of despairing women waiting outside the office of an abortionist who used nothing but these brutal techniques, Margaret Sanger in 1912 pledged to devote her life to birth control to end this misery.

The situation had not changed by 1962, when a woman described this scene, typical of the experience of millions of women: "I had to crawl through the filth of a system society had forced on me. For weeks I got on my knees to beg for help. Finally I was given a phone number in a Long Island suburb. It was a decrepit, decaying house. An old man opened the door. His shirt was stained. He spoke incoherently. Everything about him and his house disgusted me. 'You'll stay and rest overnight after the operation,' he explained, starting to paw my arm. I knew I couldn't stand it another second. I turned and ran."

A limited number of American women in the early and middle years of the twentieth century were fortunate enough to find skilled physicians practicing abortion. One such doctor, J. Bryan Henrie of Grove, Oklahoma, performed abortions along with his general practice for three decades. He helped found the public library, served as a city councilman, and was chosen Father of the Year by the PTA in 1960. "If you couldn't pay, he never said a word," one resident reported. In 1962, the death of a patient at a Tulsa hospital was presumably linked to an abortion at Dr. Henrie's clinic. When he was tried and sentenced to prison, the whole town turned out for a farewell party, many women weeping.

Since no hard statistics were available in this era of criminalization, Dr. Christopher Tietze, a leading demographer, estimated in 1957 that 200,000 to 1.2 million abortions were performed every year in the United States. By 1967 Dr. Harold Rosen, editor of the book *Therapeutic Abortion*, raised the estimate to 1.5 million.

During lengthy interviews with Margaret Sanger in 1953 and 1954 for the preparation of my biography, I often questioned her about abortion. Her knowledge was skimpy. Her emphasis had always been on contraception, and she had just recognized that recent advances in antibiotics and the vacuum technique had made abortion safe and efficient. In the late 1950s, I found that only two medical texts gave serious, if outdated, treatment of the subject. The only coverage in national magazines consisted of grim warnings about the consequences of abortion. Newspapers gave scant space to stories about the arrest and sentencing of abortionists. Indeed, abortion was the "dread secret of our society," as I wrote in 1966 in my book *Abortion*.

The subject first came to national attention in 1962 with the case of Sherri Finkbine, a television hostess at a Phoenix, Arizona, TV station, who had taken the drug thalidomide, which was prescribed as a tranquilizer and sleeping pill, after she suffered chest pains and nervous exhaustion. Finkbine later became pregnant, and at about the same time, newspapers started reporting that thalidomide could seriously damage a fetus. Frantically she sought help from a local hospital, which turned her down for an abortion after media reports led to a public debate. Finkbine and her husband were forced to fly to Sweden, which allowed abortion for limited medical reasons. The doctor told them the fetus was indeed deformed—"It was not a baby."

The subject began to haunt me. What strange twists of medical reasoning had denied Sherri Finkbine a "therapeutic abortion," as the few cases "approved" by hospital committees were then called? When a little digging revealed that abortion was completely legal in the Soviet Union and in the Eastern European countries, and legal for limited reasons in Scandinavian countries, I was puzzled as to why the fabric of American political, medical, and social dogma had blocked safe, legal abortion in the United States since the Civil War.

Even more puzzling was abortion policy in Japan. After Japan's defeat in World War II, General Douglas Mac-Arthur, who had been installed as the country's virtual dictator, legalized an extensive abortion system but ignored birth control. The reasons are obscure. Perhaps MacArthur was intent on keeping population down in this sensitive period and considered abortion far simpler and more efficient than the education and delivery network needed for contraceptive devices. There is no evidence that President Harry S. Truman was even consulted in this decision. But it seemed strange that the United States could approve abortion for a "subject" country while rejecting it at home.

In exploring religious positions on abortion, I found them slightly more advanced than state laws. The National Council of Churches, the main Protestant coalition, had approved a position in 1961 allowing hospital abortion "when the health or life of the mother is at stake." The Reform and Conservative branches of Judaism placed the health and life of the mother above that of the fetus and approved abortion for medical necessity (although Orthodox Jews opposed it). But none of these groups offered any practical definition of "health" that would determine eligibility for abortion. Most importantly, none had tried to turn their beliefs into public policy.

Considering the Roman Catholic church's current vehement opposition to abortion, its historical position is startling. Down through the centuries the church had never punished abortion as murder as long as the abortion occurred before the soul became rational or "animated," a line set at forty days after conception for the male fetus, eighty or ninety days for the female (although theologians never explained how the sex would be determined). Except for a three-year gap after 1588, the animation theory remained dogma until 1869, when Pope Pius IX suddenly abolished it, making abortion at any point murder and a sin.

All of my research drove me to write a book on the political, legal, social, and religious aspects of abortion. My first book on Margaret Sanger indicated I had a feminist bent. Three crowded years of talking and working with Sanger had completely convinced me that a woman's freedom in education, jobs, marriage, her whole life, could only be achieved when she gained control of her childbearing. I came gradually to understand that birth control required abortion as a backup measure when contraception failed or wasn't used at all. Both were integral to the right of privacy, which the U.S. Supreme Court would later establish in the *Griswold v. Connecticut* case as the basis of legalized birth control. When I finally published the book *Abortion* in 1966, I wrote: "Since the Court laid such emphasis on rights retained by the people, it might well be asked whether abortion does not fall within this category." The Court would generally accept this thesis when it legalized abortion in 1973.

It took me years of tortured debate to work out my attitudes on abortion. Even if one accepted it before quickening, as in the common law, what about abortion at six months or later, when the fetus was approaching personhood? Did the state retain any control? I, like thousands of other people, had to reach a conclusion in personal terms. If my wife ever faced this decision as a result of fetal damage, from an auto accident or a similar event, I hoped she would consult me, our family, our physician. But the ultimate choice, I decided, must be entirely hers. Even in the case of late abortion, I came to believe and insist that only the woman, not the state, should control her body, and that all prohibitive and restrictive laws on abortion must be abolished immediately.

When I put my material into an outline for a magazine article and took it to editors I had known well for years, they turned me down flat. I was told the subject was tasteless, perhaps dirty, and was warned that writing about it could possibly ruin my career. Still, I submitted the outline to book publishers in 1962 and eventually was offered a contract.

It was a lonely period. My only allies were doctors and lawyers who had just formed the Association for the Study of Abortion, whose board I joined but who wanted nothing to do with a militant stand. In California, a small, aggressive group led by Patricia Maginnis, demanded the overthrow of all abortion laws. When Lana Phelan, who became a California abortion rights leader, saw Maginnis standing on a San Francisco street corner handing out leaflets in the driving rain, she concluded: "If she could get soaked to the skin for this cause, I had to join it."

Two unexpected events occurred upon the book's completion. The incipient women's movement and the civil rights struggle seemed to have heightened the media's interest, for the *New York Times Magazine* assigned me an article on abortion, and DeWitt Wallace of *Reader's Digest*, long a partisan of Margaret Sanger, decided to run a condensed version of the book in early 1966. Despite the national attention brought by such powerful media, I was afraid no one would show up for a press conference at publication. Instead, the room was jammed with TV cameras and radio and newspaper reporters. I was flooded with requests for interviews and toured the country. Everywhere I went, women would gather and form abortion rights groups, which would soon become the backbone of a national movement.

The turning point came when a reporter asked: "Since you want the unlimited right of abortion, what are you going to do about it?" I had met a few doctors performing skilled abortion, such as Henrie, Robert Spenser in Pennsylvania, Milan Vuitch in Washington, D.C. "I'll send women to skilled doctors," I replied, "and test the constitutionality of the laws." In that moment, everything changed. I had turned from a writer into a militant activist. The movement called it "confrontation politics." When the Reverend Howard Moody and the Clergy Consultation Service began similar referrals a few years later, we alerted the country to the plight of women and the difference between high medical standards and the back-room abortionist.

It was a risky movement. Despite paid bookings, Maginnis and Phelan had halls canceled at the last minute after boycotts and pickets in Albuquerque, New Mexico, and Milwaukee, Wisconsin. Members of the Clergy Service were indicted, and pursued for extradition to other states for trial. Maginnis and Bill Baird, a Long Island activist, were jailed. Moody and I were called before the Bronx Grand Jury and grilled.

Still, by 1967, we were able to pass three new abortion laws in Colorado, North Carolina, and California. They were a modest step, following the formula of the American Law Institute (ALI) by generally broadening indications for abortion from "saving life" to "preserving health," but maintaining a complex system of approval by hospital committees. Only a few thousand women each year in each state could surmount these hurdles. Ironically, in California, Governor Ronald Reagan signed the bill into law.

By the summer of 1968 the movement had grown strong enough for five militants to meet in New York City to plan a national organization. At the founding meeting in Chicago in February 1969, the critical debate concerned whether the organization would follow the ALI formula of modest reform or aim for total repeal of all restrictive abortion laws. The repeal position won handily, and the National Association for Repeal of Abortion Laws (NARAL), with myself as chairman, became a coalition of national groups like the American Public Health Association, along with state and local NARAL chapters. After the Supreme Court legalized abortion in 1973, the organization's name was changed to the National Abortion Rights Action League.

Our founding strategy had two prongs: not just state legislation overthrowing the old laws, but court challenges that might accomplish the same ends. In California, Dr. Leon Belous, an eminent obstetrician-gynecologist, openly announced in early 1967 that he was referring patients for abortion. After his indictment and trial, the state supreme court in September 1969 exonerated him and ruled that the prohibitory state law was unconstitutional. Soon 135,000 abortions would be done annually at California clinics and doctors' offices.

In Washington, Dr. Milan Vuitch followed our plan to keep detailed records on the health status of every woman who came to him for an abortion. When he was indicted and tried in federal court, Judge Arnold Gesell not only exonerated him but ruled that a "woman's liberty and right of privacy extends to family, marriage, and sex matters and may well include the right to remove an unwanted child, at least in early stages of pregnancy," words that undoubtedly had an impact on the Supreme Court in 1973.

The big push would come in New York in 1970. Although 40 percent of the state's population was Catholic, and the church had built a seemingly invincible lobby at the state capital, our strategy depended on a two-party coalition. Constance Cook, a Republican, and Franz Leichter, a Democrat, guided a strong bill through the assembly. NARAL, church groups, and medical groups campaigned in every district, concentrating on wavering Catholics. "State Senator Edward Speno (a Nassau Republican and Catholic) and many other legislators learned that public demand for abortion repeal was at a point where they couldn't vote No," reported State Senator Manfred Ohrenstein.

On the Senate side, the majority leader, a Catholic, submitted an abortion bill so radical he was sure no one could support it. Surprisingly, his strategy failed. The bill passed. Suddenly frantic, the Catholic lobby turned all its power on the assembly. Delegations, including bishops and priests, pressured Catholic members of the assembly like Mary Anne Krupsak and picketed their offices. When the vote was called on April 9, it remained a tie (or defeat) till the end. Then George Michaels, an upstate Democratic assemblyman, took the podium, announcing that he would switch his vote from No to Yes even though it was certain to ruin his political career. The bill passed, and although it did not completely repeal all abortion laws, it allowed abortion through twenty-four weeks of pregnancy—the most sweeping legislation in the country and a landmark in abortion rights.

As Alaska, Hawaii, and other states passed similar laws in the next few years, two legal challenges to prohibitive statutes (among many in the federal courts) moved toward the Supreme Court. On January 22, 1973, the Court delivered its opinion in *Roe v. Wade* from Texas and *Doe v. Bolton* from Georgia. By a 7 to 2 vote in both cases, the Court legalized abortion throughout the country virtually to the point where the fetus became viable. It seemed almost a miracle. Seven years before, abortion rights depended on a dozen militants. But in that short period abortion had galvanized the women's movement, the family planning movement, medical, legal, and social welfare organizations, and state and local chapters of

NARAL into a coalition that produced a social revolution faster than any other in U.S. history.

For younger men and women, who have grown up considering abortion rights an inalienable right that has always existed, the counterattack often seems like an aberration of American politics. Yet it was carefully planned and constructed. The first phase started in 1975 when the National Conference of Catholic Bishops issued its Pastoral Plan for Pro-Life Activities, aimed at turning every parish and every Catholic organization in the country into a political instrument that would wipe out abortion rights. The second phase was launched in 1979 when the Fundamentalist Crusade Against Abortion joined the Catholic church in an alliance that made religion a national force in politics. The presidential elections of 1980, 1984, and 1988, which put Ronald Reagan and George Bush in the White House, not only produced anti-abortion administrations but guaranteed that the federal courts would soon be dominated by conservative and mainly anti-abortion judges.

It may seem puzzling that the Catholic church and religious Fundamentalists have made abortion their dominant issue. Targeting pro-choice candidates, they defeated U.S. Senator Richard Clark in Iowa in 1978, among many others. In 1980 Catholic parishes openly supported political candidates in violation of First Amendment separation of church and state. In 1984 Cardinal Bernard Law of Boston called abortion the "critical issue of this campaign." Violence soon became integral to the anti-abortion campaign. At a 1984 conference for teaching methods of eliminating abortion clinics, Joseph Scheidler, a former Benedictine monk, announced that

"I have yet to shed my first tear when I see a charred abortion clinic."

In trying to explain Cardinal Law's obsession with abortion, William V. Shannon, a former ambassador to Ireland and a Catholic himself, defined Law's fear that "if you don't draw the line here, then everything becomes permissible." If the Catholic-Fundamentalist campaign against abortion represents part of a total campaign against pornography, homosexuality, sexual freedom, and every issue labeled "secular humanism," then the very social cohesiveness of America becomes threatened. The pluralist design of the First Amendment, which allows every moral and religious belief to have full sway, may be eroded and eventually crushed.

Above all, the right to privacy is at stake here. More than any other factor, the introduction of the abortion pill RU 486 into the United States could guarantee the right to privacy by placing abortion in a doctor's office, with no one but the woman and her doctor aware of the procedure. In comparing the slavery issue before the Civil War with the abortion issue, I wrote in 1973: "Both involved fundamental moral and religious positions that collided with the entrenched interests of their time." The portents for divisiveness were ominous in 1973, but are even more ominous today. If RU 486 can help to allay this increasing discord, its availability becomes critical for all women and men in this country.

Part One
The Significance of RU 486

1

RU 486: "The Moral Property of Women"

Rarely in history has a scientific discovery had the power to intervene in the religious and political conflicts of our time. Scientific and technological innovations have radically altered our lives, hurtling us faster through space, speeding communications, expanding information. Still, these advances have rarely altered the relationships between men and women, nor have they affected the strength, and even the survival, of families.

Such an impact, following previous advances in contraception, may be produced by a new pill developed in France, known scientifically as mifepristone but generally called RU 486. Approved for public use by the French government (and the Chinese government), RU 486 has induced abortion before the ninth week of pregnancy for more than fifty thousand French women. In 1991, the pill is expected to be approved for public use in Great Britain, the Netherlands, and three Scandinavian countries. Claude Evin, the French minister of health, has hailed it as the "moral property of women." Dr. Ian Mackenzie, a leading British researcher, has rated his country's testing results as "fantastic."

Two of the new pill's important attributes are its effectiveness and safety. The pill, which has virtually no side effects, has induced abortion successfully in 96 percent of all cases. In those rare instances when it fails, women must choose to have a standard vacuum abortion. The crowning achievement of RU 486, however, is that it gives women the option of more privacy in their childbearing decisions. Only the woman and her doctor need ever know that she has taken the pill, and followed it with an injection or suppository a day or two later. Women do not need an institutional setting since they only experience bleeding similar to if slightly heavier than their menstrual flow, bleeding described by medical experts as "slightly more than their normal period."

The increased privacy afforded by RU 486 and the lack of physical invasion of the body enhance the psychological environment of abortion. As shown by the French experience, many women have demonstrated they still prefer the one-step, quick procedure of vacuum aspiration. Yet despite the impressive safety record of aspiration, some women will always dislike the clinical surroundings of treatment rooms staffed with gowned and masked doctors and nurses, surroundings that are part of a clinic or hospital abortion. In addition, there are the inconvenience and the occasional risk of local or general anesthesia. All of these clinical aspects of abortion have been eliminated with RU 486, which gives the woman full control over her abortion in the surroundings of her choice.

It is hardly surprising that 77 percent of French women who have undergone both vacuum and RU 486 abortion favored the pill. Of the first 103 cases studied by Dr. Mackenzie in Britain, more than 80 percent of the women said they would opt for the pill if they had another abortion.

RU 486 presents a classic case of how scientific progress can revolutionize our lives. Within the last century, the railroad opened up Western America and became a major factor in turning the United States into an economic colossus. The elevator was essential to the development of the skyscraper, the vertical city, and the concentration of business and services in a unified geographic area. The automobile gave us more than speed; it opened up the suburbs and the possibility of combining a rural or semirural life-style with employment in the central city. The cathode-ray tube made television possible. Antibiotics and other pioneering drugs extended our life span and improved the quality of these added years.

But when it comes to making an impact on our personal relationships, the science of controlling human reproduction must be considered unique. No other development—not even the telephone, with its advantage of bringing families and friends together—has so drastically changed our lives. The steady advance of contraceptive methods, from the condom and the diaphragm to the birth control pill, has redefined the nature of the family. Men and women, previously powerless to control childbearing, can now make a conscious decision about the number and spacing of their offspring. Women have been freed from the burden of unwanted pregnancies and given the freedom to plan their educational and career goals. The experience of sexuality itself has been raised to a plane of mutual pleasure, no longer an act laden with the fear of devastating consequences.

It was science again that produced safe and efficient abortion as a backup to guarantee childbearing decisions. When Margaret Sanger started campaigning for birth control in 1912, abortion was fraught with danger even in the hands of a skilled physician. A woman's uterus could be punctured, resulting in a serious infection and often death. This was particularly the case while punitive laws forced most women to seek the help of hack, back-alley practitioners. Abortion, as an emergency measure in case contraception failed or was used incorrectly or not used at all, was not socially, medically, and legally accepted until two medical advances were made. After World War II, antibiotics virtually eliminated the risk of infection, and by the 1960s, doctors had made the technique of vacuum aspiration, developed in China, far safer and more efficient than dilatation and curettage by instrument.

With the development of RU 486, scientific progress has reached a new stage. RU 486 not only eliminates the need for surgery and minimizes the negative impact on the hormonal system of the birth control pill, but it could move the setting of abortion to the privacy of a doctor's office and keep reproductive choice totally within the control of doctor and patient. It is these elements of privacy and control that have galvanized the women's and family planning movements to campaign for the approval of RU 486 in the United States. Because it returns control to women with the protection of privacy, RU 486 promises to end the furious political clash over abortion. Obviously, once RU 486 becomes available in the United States, opponents of abortion cannot picket or raid every doctor's office in the country or identify every woman who might be seeking to end her pregnancy. RU 486 thus introduces both a medical advance and a powerful new weapon that could alter the whole nature of the abortion struggle.

Well aware that this new pill could cripple their drive to outlaw abortion rights, anti-abortion forces have sworn to ban it from the United States and boycott any drug company that manufactures or distributes it here. The National Right to Life Committee has labeled it a "death drug," and Fundamentalists have called it a "human pesticide." As a result of the Catholic-Fundamentalist alliance with the White House, Presidents Reagan and Bush both have stopped all RU 486 research on abortion at the National Institutes of Health and have forced the U.S. Food and Drug Administration (FDA) to put the pill on the proscribed list, blocking its entry into the country. U.S. Representative Robert Dornan (R-Cal.) has introduced legislation to prohibit RU 486 and prevent its approval by the FDA.

Consequently, RU 486 has stepped up the peculiar vehemence of American abortion politics, which for several years has threatened to divide this country like no other issue since slavery. In fact, no other industrialized nation has come close to the United States in political divisiveness over abortion. Each U.S. election raises the pitch of anger. Cardinal John O'Connor of New York recently rated abortion the "most important issue of our day." It may be the ultimate irony that before admission of the pill to the United States the French manufacturer of RU 486 considers distributing it in Italy and Spain, both predominantly Catholic countries and Spain only fifteen years after Franco's fascism.

We are increasingly obsessed with "what may or may not be done with the womb," observes Russell Baker, a *New York Times* columnist. "At this stage of political development the womb becomes a species of public domain, a miniature Yellowstone Park, as it were, inside every woman, who is subject to arrest by park rangers if she disobeys the regulations."

Opponents of abortion want the most drastic regulations: outlawing of abortion nationwide through a U.S. Supreme Court decision, or by local legislation in individual states—Pennsylvania, for example, has passed anti-abortion laws. They are equally determined to curtail abortion through parental-notification requirements for teenagers, or through subterfuges that would forbid abortion as a substitute for birth control—in effect, wiping it out.

Still, violence remains the main instrument of the extremist right wing, particularly the group calling itself "Operation Rescue."

While the right to picket abortion sites under the First Amendment must be scrupulously protected, the thirty-four bombings of abortion providers from 1977 through 1989, the forty-seven cases of arson, and the thirty-nine cases of attempted bombing and arson make up a frightening record of illegality.

In a concerted plan to disrupt the abortion system, extremists invaded and vandalized clinics 243 times in that period, often causing hundreds of thousands of dollars' worth of damage. They have blocked entrances and chained themselves to furniture inside, depriving some patients of their constitutional right to an abortion and other patients of their access to services such as sex education and contraception. They have pushed and struck patients to stop their entry, tracked patients to their homes through auto license plate numbers, broken windows and defaced patients' property with piles of garbage, and harassed them with obscene phone calls and letters.

The medical profession has suffered an equally dangerous impact. The harassment and boycotting of doctors has forced many to stop not only practicing abortion, but offering contraceptive services and voluntary sterilization as well. It is not uncommon for doctors to move to another city or town under such pressure, often leaving an area with a shortage of medical care. The religious zealotry of Operation Rescue is reflected in the credo of its founder, Randall Terry: "If you believe abortion is murder, you must act like it is murder." Assuming the role of a fiery prophet, he warns: "We as a nation are doomed to a severe chastening from the hand of God."

Yet Terry himself represents the family divisions, as well as the political divisions, that abortion has produced. Two of his aunts are dedicated feminists, one of them the former communications director at the Planned Parenthood chapter in Rochester, New York. A Catholic family I know, similar to many others, according to Catholics for a Free Choice, is so split between advocates of abortion rights and anti-abortionists that arguments and anger at dinner have made the celebration of Christmas and Easter almost impossible.

Since polls have shown that hard-core Catholics against all abortion rights make up only 15 to 20 percent of Catholics, RU 486 could have a considerable influence on moderate Catholics and Fundamentalists too. Opposition has always been based on the religious conviction that human personhood begins at the moment of conception. Abortion, therefore, constitutes murder. The intensity of this conviction has been bolstered by the display of pictures and models of a fetus at twelve weeks' or longer gestation, at which point it bears some physical features of an infant at the time of delivery.

But RU 486 works at such an early stage that moderate opponents of abortion might be persuaded to reexamine their objections in light of the drug's biological significance. When a woman taking the pill produces only a heavy menstrual flow, there is absolutely no sign of personhood, nothing even resembling a potential finger or toe. What, then, could a moderate observer think has been "killed"? In fact, it would be hard to differentiate the pill's action from a "miscarriage," a normal event (scientists call it nature's own method of weeding out the less hardy products of conception) that happens to most women once or many times in their lives. Miscarriage occurs so frequently that women often fail to realize it has taken place.

Dr. Étienne-Émile Baulieu, one of the prime developers of the pill in France, consequently insists that the effect of RU 486 should not be called abortion at all but rather "contragestion," a contraction of the word "contragestation." He stresses that there are "several steps that are critical for the proper development of the embryo." He describes the generation of life as a "continuous process that involves interdependent sequential events that cannot be attributed uniquely to fertilization," and concludes: "Considering the process of generating life, in its globality and continuity, and the natural, selective mechanisms that determine existence, the use of the terms *murder* and *killing* in relation to abortion cloud the real issues pertaining to an existing health problem."

RU 486 thus brings to the debate a new dimension for moderate Catholics and Fundamentalists to consider. The pill's action involves body chemistry, not surgical intervention. Resembling miscarriage, it simply sheds early embryonic development during a brief period of slightly heavy bleeding followed by a lighter flow that lasts about a week. Referring to the fetus at this early stage, Dr. David Grimes, who has tested RU 486 at the University of Southern California, explains, "You can't even find it."

Perhaps the most disturbing aspect of the extremist frenzy against RU 486 is that scientists are hindered in their development of many secondary uses of the compound that could revolutionize a whole range of medical treatments. The pill has proved valuable for limiting the growth of brain tumors and relieving symptoms of Cushing's syndrome, a life-threatening condition that results from excessive production of adrenal gland hormone. It has been tested for use in the treatment of breast cancer and endometrial cancer; it may even be instrumental in the production of a simpler and more efficient form of contraception than the present birth control pill. By stopping the entry of RU 486 into the United States, extremists are obstructing far more than an advanced abortion method. They are blocking essential medical research, thus denying thousands of people the benefits of more effective treatments and improved health.

RU 486 could, in addition, bring immense advantages to underdeveloped nations. Contraception and voluntary sterilization are in such short supply in most areas that an estimated 500 million couples and individuals lack effective means of fertility control. Most women, therefore, are pushed into the hands of the crudest purveyors of back-alley abortions, and more than 200,000 women die each year from botched attempts, according to statistics gathered by the World Health Organization. RU 486 could contribute greatly to ending this needless loss of human life. Admittedly, doctors and hospitals are scarce in the third world, but networks of trained paramedicals could administer the pill with hospital backup, much as paramedicals have been trained to perform menstrual regulation, a form of abortion, in Bangladesh. Yet few international organizations, nor the Roussel Uclaf Company itself, have concentrated on finding a solution that would adapt the Bangladesh system to the administration of RU 486 in poor countries.

Worldwide population control could be an indirect benefit of the use of RU 486. Women must always control the choice of bearing or not bearing a child, but when that choice is made safer, more efficient, and more acceptable, chaotically expanding populations will naturally be reduced to more manageable proportions. World population passed the five billion mark in 1987, and since then has surged at the rate of eighty million more people each year. Most of this increase occurs in countries already desperate to provide minimal food, housing, and sanitation for its people. With the World Health Organization warning that the "balance between man and nature [is] already in serious jeopardy and the entire future of mankind at stake," RU 486 could become a critical factor in slowing down the torrent of human reproduction.

The ultimate irony involving the use of RU 486 in the

United States is that scientists at the FDA, which is responsible for approving any new drug, have already studied thousands of French cases and have given the data unofficially the highest rating. The compound's introduction into the United States however, will depend not on its medical safety, but on the political climate. RU 486, perhaps more than any drug in our history, will reach the public through votes and political clout rather than through scrutiny for safety and effectiveness.

The absurdity of this situation, in the long run, may benefit the pro-choice movement by giving it a special focus for its anger and energies. Once the women and men of America understand the crucial issue of privacy inherent in RU 486, the White House and its extremist allies may rue their decision to block it from the country. If the admission of RU 486 cannot be secured through normal channels, the women's movement will ineluctably develop other strategies for its entry, even if only into a few states at first. These strategies to introduce the drug will certainly be tested in the courts, and will produce a momentous legal challenge. Even the wavering center in the abortion struggle, along with moderate Catholics, may become convinced that a woman's privacy in the doctor-patient relationship should overrule all other considerations. The issue of privacy may become the real battleground of the feminist future, the arena for the final struggle that establishes RU 486 as the "moral property of women."

—— **2** ——

The Making of RU 486

Science has a tendency to glamorize its heroes, perhaps pressured by the public and the media to oversimplify their achievements. Many discoveries, like the polio vaccine, consequently have become identified with a single name. In the case of RU 486, Dr. Étienne-Émile Baulieu, a member of the French Academy of Sciences, has gained this distinction. *Science* magazine has labeled Baulieu "chief developer" of the pill, and the prestigious journal *Nature* has reported that he "discovered" the pill. In truth Baulieu does little to refute these claims, often giving the "impression that he's alone in this work," as one scientist observes.

While Baulieu played a critical role in the development of RU 486, and has virtually made a career of dashing anywhere from New York to Rio de Janeiro to lobby for its acceptance, an over simplified focus on one person ignores the fact that RU 486 was made possible through the work of a team of researchers. Scientists are hardly immune to the pressures of politics and the lure of celebrity, and the development of RU 486 involves a weave of claims and counterclaims that is often difficult to unravel. We must also take into account the evolutionary process that underlies every discovery, a chain of building blocks going back many decades.

The first insight into the concept behind RU 486 appears in the work of Dr. Gregory Pincus, one of Baulieu's mentors, an expert on steroids, and the man who developed the birth control pill in the 1950s at the Worcester Foundation for Experimental Biology in Massachusetts. Grasping the importance of "receptor tissue" in his 1962 experiments on rats and mice, Pincus theorized that "antiprogestins should be implantation inhibitors" by acting on the specific receptors, located mainly in the nuclei of cells in the uterus and stopping the growth of the egg. This is basically what RU 486 would accomplish.

Baulieu first formed links to Pincus in 1961. Already a promising young scientist, Baulieu came to New York from France that year to work on steroids under Professor Seymour Lieberman, a prominent Columbia University biochemist. Baulieu was already exhibiting his independent style. He was a protégé of Professor M. F. Jayle, the dominant teacher of French biochemistry. In this period, few scientists left Paris, which was considered the hub of their universe, but "Baulieu always went his own way," Lieberman recalls.

Lieberman's friendship with Pincus would also have an impact on Baulieu's career. Baulieu sought to use science as an expression of social responsibility. "I wanted my work in the lab to apply to people's suffering," he stated. After Lieberman introduced Baulieu to Pincus, the Worcester scientist took Baulieu to Puerto Rico, where the birth control pill was being tested. Once Baulieu realized that birth control was pivotal to women's health and the control of world population—which was pro-

jected to grow by one billion people every twenty years—
he committed himself to steroid research, the basis of
chemical contraception.

One of the first breakthrough discoveries opening the
way for the development of RU 486 had occurred in 1932
when a German chemist established the chemical structure of steroids, the sex hormones controlling male and
female reproduction. Over the next few years, different
groups of German, Swiss, and U.S. chemists identified a
whole range of steroids, including estradiol, progesterone, and testosterone.

The catalytic force that eventually pushed steroid research toward a social application came from Margaret
Sanger, the tireless campaigner for birth control. Convinced by her medical associate, Dr. Abraham Stone, that
steroids might provide a contraceptive pill more efficient
and acceptable than the diaphragm or condom, Sanger
investigated every lead. She went to Russia in 1934 to
observe one steroid experiment, but this search and others turned up nothing. It was not until 1951 that Stone
and Sanger decided that work at the Worcester Foundation promised a potential breakthrough. By 1952 she was
already raising millions of dollars to support Pincus's research.

Another important breakthrough necessary for the development of RU 486 was the synthesizing of sex hormones in the laboratory for mass production. Natural
hormones from animals were inordinately expensive. A
tiny amount of estrogen estradiol, for example, had to be
drawn from thousands of gallons of urine from pregnant
mares. But in the early 1940s, Professor Russell E. Marker
of Pennsylvania State University discovered how to syn-

thesize 3,000 grams of progesterone (then worth eighty dollars a gram) from the common Mexican yam. In 1944, the Syntex Company was established in Mexico City to market the process, and the chemist, Dr. Carl Djerassi, perfected the synthesis of cortisone, progesterone, and other sex hormones from yam-derived steroids.

Syntex soon became the leading supplier of synthetic steroids, not just for Pincus's research, but for commercial use for many drug companies that developed birth control pills after 1960. RU 486 is in fact, a synthetically changed form of norethindrone, a progestin used in the birth control pill, which was developed and patented by Syntex in 1951. But RU 486 is antagonistic to progesterone. By occupying the space in the progesterone receptor without activating it, RU 486 impedes progesterone from entering the receptor. Instead of inducing the usual hormone responses, RU 486 stops them.

Progesterone, a sex steroid, plays a central role in the establishment and maintenance of pregnancy. It prepares the uterus for implantation and nurtures the egg. Receptors in the uterus receive the progesterone (there is a specific receptor for each hormone). If fertilization occurs, progesterone production helps the new embryo lodge in the lining of the uterus. It promotes the development of the placenta, relaxes the uterine muscle to decrease contractions that might expel an embryo, and firms the cervix, preventing its dilation.

Normally, when progesterone locks into the receptor, all these biological processes are triggered. But RU 486, an anti-progestin, takes the space of progesterone without activating the process. Thus it "barricades" the receptor. Receptors are like magnets, recognizing the chemical affinity of progesterone (or other hormones) and exerting a binding force. When RU 486 penetrates the receptor, it binds to it and deceives it, working against implantation. The developing placenta and embryo detach from the uterine lining. The corpus luteum (a progesterone gland) starts to decay. Without progesterone action, there is increased contractility of the uterine muscle, softening the dilation of the cervix, and contractions that dislodge and expel the embryo. Thus, through the seventh to ninth weeks of the woman's cycle, RU 486 brings about an early abortion mainly because of diminished progesterone and bleeding that results from shedding of the endometrium (the mucous membrane lining the uterus).

Baulieu's most important contribution to the development of RU 486 was his work involving the chemical composition of the receptor. Still, the accumulation of prior research made it possible for him to solve the final puzzle. Paul Ehrlich in 1909 postulated the existence of hormone receptors and gave them their name. Professor Elwood V. Jensen of the University of Chicago defined the uterine receptor specifically at a Vienna conference in 1958, and in research published over the next ten years analyzed "target tissues" of the uterus and their "unique components" called receptors. In his 1969 and 1970 studies, Professor Bert O'Malley, then of Vanderbilt University School of Medicine, reported on baby chicks' uterine receptors, "a specific target for progesterone," and the binding action of progestins.

When Baulieu started progesterone receptor research around 1970, he insists that "no one knew then how the receptor really functioned." His work at his laboratories at Bicêtre Hospital in Paris was being funded by the Institut National de la Santé et Recherche Médicale (INSERM), a government agency. During this time, Jean Claude Roussel, a son of the founder of Roussel Uclaf, offered Baulieu a job as director of research. "You don't know what it is to become rich," Baulieu was told. He turned down the job offer, however, choosing instead to become an exclusive consultant to the drug company.

As research proceeded, Baulieu developed a paper, published in 1970, showing that the "binding system responds to some of the criteria of what is usually called a hormone receptor" in animal tests, but the "difference in the binding of progesterone in the uteri of different species" was still "puzzling."

Roussel at this early stage was actually looking for an anti-cortisone compound. A research group in Roussel's endocrinology department, headed by Dr. Georges Teutsch, was trying to develop the best molecule close to cortisone, which is similar to progesterone, a molecule that would bind to and block the receptors without triggering the normal hormonal response. A steroid or sex hormone is like a key, and an anti-steroid can prevent the key from opening the lock. In essence, Baulieu's work was defining the shape of the lock, while Teutsch and his group were making a fake key that would fit the lock. By occupying the lock, a fake key would impede the real key from opening the door.

Using highly specific radioactivity to identify hormones and study their action without altering their normal function, Teutsch in the early 1970s was measuring the binding strength of a range of steroidal compounds. "Chemistry is like building a house," he explained. "You can play with molecules, replacing them, adding to them. We were looking for the best steroid that could be modified to block the cortisone receptor."

Although Baulieu and Teutsch would confer occasionally at Roussel, their research was essentially independent, and each group published its own papers. In 1974, Daniel Philibert and J. P. Raynaud at Roussel described how a "highly potent synthetic progestin," developed by Roussel and labeled R 5020, worked on the receptors of guinea pigs, rabbits, rats, and mice, and reported that a "comparable progestin receptor is to be found in the human uterus."

That same year, Dr. Edouard Sakiz (soon to become the company president), Raynaud, and others at Roussel tested R 2323, a similar compound, on animals and eventually on one hundred women, and found that if administered monthly, it could produce an "effective form of contraception" through its progesterone-binding effect. But Roussel management, still looking for an anticortisone, was uninterested in birth control. Not only was testing expensive, but a new birth control pill probably would not make much of a dent in an overcrowded market.

The exact point at which Baulieu at INSERM or the Teutsch group at Roussel began to concentrate on abortion is difficult to pin down. In a 1975 paper, Baulieu urged more research on the "relationship between receptor concentration and hormone action." A year later, Sakiz, Raynaud, and others at Roussel reported that R 2323 "might prevent progesterone-induced changes and consequently implantation."

This was a major step toward an abortion compound,

but Roussel's management kept the focus on anti-cortisone development, and allowed the Teutsch group to study only glucocorticoids, which are cortisones. Over the next few years, Teutsch tested hundreds of compounds for anti-cortisone effects. "We wanted one with the highest binding qualities," Teutsch recalled. Starting with chemical tests, the Teutsch group then used the compounds on tissue culture *in vitro* and eventually on animals. In 1980, Teutsch told a meeting of Roussel executives that some compounds had real potential as a new abortifacient.

All told, nine hundred compounds may have been screened. "It took a shotgun approach," is how a scientist at the National Institutes of Health described the group's method. Another scientist referred to the chemists' "stumbling" onto an anti-progesterone while looking for an anti-cortisone. In response, Teutsch and Philibert wrote the American Association for the Advancement of Science on December 12, 1989, that "discovery of the properties of RU 486 and the related class of compounds is the logical result of a very classical research approach . . ."

The compound that Roussel finally decided to promote was called mifepristone, or RU 486, which exhibited the highest binding affinity to the receptor and thus completely blocked the action of natural progesterone. Roussel applied for a patent in 1980, and it was approved the next year. The patent bore the names of Teutsch, Philibert, and others in the group, but not that of Baulieu. But Baulieu's influence on Sakiz, then a company vice president, cannot be underestimated. Baulieu had recommended Sakiz for a job at Roussel. Baulieu was undoubtedly responsible for convincing the company to start testing RU 486 on animals as an abortifacient, and in 1982, he launched tests on humans.

Baulieu approached Professor Walter Hermann of Geneva's University Hospital, an old friend from their days in New York with Lieberman, and got him to search for women volunteers. Eleven pregnant women agreed to participate in the first test, and after administration of RU 486, nine aborted quickly. The other two had to be given vacuum abortions.

Following another year of testing on small groups, Baulieu called a press conference and announced that RU 486 would be on the market in a few years. The prestige he had gained by election to the French Academy of Sciences in 1983, largely from his work on steroids, certainly contributed to the resulting media attention. It remains unclear whether Roussel approved the press conference, but the company had undoubtedly seized on Baulieu's flair for publicity to spearhead a public relations campaign for the pill. Teutsch and his associates, however, were furious, and complained to management that Baulieu's timetable for release of the pill was highly premature.

As researchers in Britain, Sweden, and other countries obtained RU 486 from Roussel for their own local tests, Baulieu in 1986 reported on the first major sample of 100 women. RU 486 achieved a success rate of 85 percent with no damaging side effects. In another test sample of 340 women seeking an early abortion, only 2 women had to receive abortions by the vacuum method.

An international network of scientists now became involved in testing programs in many countries—Dr. Marc Bygdeman at Karolinska Hospital in Stockholm; Dr. David

Baird at the University of Edinburgh; Dr. Ian Mackenzie at Oxford University; Drs. David Grimes and D. R. Mishell at the University of Southern California in Los Angeles. Determined to eliminate the scourge of botched abortions in poor countries, the World Health Organization set up thirteen test sites, including Hungary, India, and Yugoslavia.

One objective of the tests was to find an effective dosage of RU 486, which was finally set at 600 milligrams. Another concern was to increase efficacy. Bygdeman had done pioneering research on prostaglandins—substances in body tissue that act like hormones and as intermediaries in the metabolic process. He demonstrated that a small dose, given by injection or vaginal suppository, would make the uterus react more strongly than with RU 486 alone. Bleeding would be decreased, uterine contractions stimulated. As a result, abortion often occurred within a few hours. "The combined therapy," Bygdeman and his associates reported, was "more effective than RU 486 alone."

By 1988, the success rate of RU 486 had been raised to 95 or 96 percent, a figure bolstered by the results of tests on 2,115 women in France. After the prostaglandin dose, 96 percent completed their abortions within twenty-four hours. Fewer than 1 percent had heavy bleeding, and only one woman had to be given a blood transfusion. Complications from bleeding were no more frequent than in vacuum abortion. Incomplete abortions amounted to just 2.1 percent.

Scientists in every test country agree that the next logical step should be a delayed-action dose of prostaglandin combined with RU 486 in one pill or injection. But here the politics of the drug industry has intervened. Although several countries make different prostaglandins, the French health system prefers the injectable type, and the Schering Company of West Germany holds the principal patent. Schering also happens to have patents on lilopristone (ZK 98.734) and onapristone (ZK 98.299), compounds that virtually duplicate the action of RU 486 but have not been marketed.

Furthermore, Schering holds a patent for the combined use of any anti-progestin combined with a prostaglandin. This gives Schering a bargaining chip in its negotiations with Roussel for the prostaglandin patent, but Sakiz denies this. "We have no patent problems with Schering," he insists.

Although tests soon proved that RU 486 stayed in the body for several days, no other receptors were affected except for a weak anti-cortisone action. Consequently, experience has shown that women have been able to conceive again shortly after undergoing an RU 486 abortion.

In addition, researchers were concerned that RU 486 would damage a fetus in the cases of the minuscule number of women who failed to end their pregnancies with the pill, rejected a vacuum abortion, and brought the fetus to term. This is theoretically possible. Therefore, doctors urge that if the abortion is incomplete, a vacuum aspiration be carried out. Nevertheless, a few women have changed their minds and decided to continue pregnancy after taking RU 486. One fetal deformity showed up after eighteen weeks, but studies demonstrated that it probably resulted from causes other than RU 486. "Strictly speaking," concluded Professor Roger Henrion of the

Hospital of Paris, "there has been no case of a malformed baby born to a mother who has taken RU 486 during pregnancy."

Thousands of successful tests had proved the safety and effectiveness of RU 486. Roussel submitted this data to the French Ministry of Health, and after intensive evaluation, the pill was officially approved for public use on September 23, 1988. In France the approval of a drug rests solely on its medical and scientific merits. In the United States approval may be controlled more by politicians than by scientists. The Food and Drug Administration (FDA) is the creature of the Secretary of Health and Human Services, who in turn is a creature of the White House. Although leading scientists at the FDA consider the French data sufficient basis for American approval, the Catholic-Fundamentalist-White House coalition against RU 486 has been so strident that the Roussel Company has not even considered starting the FDA application process.

The approval of RU 486 in France brought an immediate international reaction. Family planning experts hailed the approval, while abortion opponents, especially the Catholic church in France, denounced the decision. The Catholic church was well aware that RU 486 could critically weaken its anti-abortion campaign.

3

The People and Politics of RU 486

Politics has dominated the development of RU 486 almost as much as research. It has become the most controversial drug in decades, the center of governmental debates, the focus of intense campaigns in Europe and the United States over its approval or rejection for public use. Inside the Roussel Company itself, RU 486 has created similar acrimony, with scientists making competing claims for the credit for its discovery.

No one has played a more critical part in this uproar than Dr. Edouard Sakiz, president of Roussel. He has been forced to become a mediator of company passions and public policy, an executive who would influence national health choices as well as the direction of a giant drug manufacturer. In the disputes surrounding RU 486, the most ironic aspect is that Dr. Baulieu originally introduced Sakiz to the company, and this would never be forgotten by Roussel's staff.

After Sakiz rose to become head of the company's biological research laboratories, Jean-Claude Roussel, son of the founder, recognized his talents for management, and offered him an executive post. Sakiz protested that he was a "pure scientist." Roussel argued, "You are successful and you are lucky. You know how to deal with people." When Roussel was killed in an accident in 1974, Sakiz was promoted to general manager, a few years later to vice president, and to president in 1981. It seemed almost destined that Sakiz's skill at mediation would guide the company through the RU 486 crisis.

Founded in 1920, the Roussel Company has become the most important steroid producer in the world. It has subsidiaries in thirty countries and partnerships in sixty more. It makes agricultural, chemical, medical, cosmetic, and nutritional products, but concentrates on health care and pharmaceuticals for future growth. After Roussel's death, the Hoechst Corporation of West Germany bought most of the stock, but in 1982 the French government bought back 36.25 percent, leaving Hoechst with 54.5 percent and a few remaining shares on the public market.

Sitting behind a massive desk at the company's headquarters only a few blocks from Napoleon's tomb at Les Invalides, Sakiz has surrounded himself with sculptures and paintings that make his office almost a miniature museum. His strawberry-blond hair has thinned to the point of baldness, but he remains lithe and dapper. Born in Istanbul of Armenian ancestry in 1926, he took his medical degree and his doctoral degree in science in Paris, and became professor of endocrinology at the Collège de France. His fluency in English comes from three years of teaching physiology at the Baylor College of Medicine in Texas. His thesis was on the adrenal cortex, but the research phase of his career has now been replaced by a bevy of executive assistants, secretaries, and other trappings of power that crowd the floor of his office.

Dr. Georges Teutsch, director of the endocrinology department that worked on RU 486, comes closer to the stereotype of a research scientist than Sakiz. He speaks slowly and quietly. His gold-rimmed glasses and thinning, graying hair add to his scholarly aura. Born in Alsace in 1941 of German descent, he got his doctoral degree from the University of Nancy. After working two years for Schering in New Jersey, where his English was perfected, he decided that industry offered the best opportunity for research and joined Roussel. He reads Schopenhauer extensively. He has climbed peaks everywhere, including the Grand Tetons of Wyoming.

Daniel Philibert, Teutsch's close associate, was born in Algeria in 1940, the third generation of French settlers. After taking his degree in biophysics in Morocco, he joined Roussel in 1967. Big and slightly beefy, he has kept an innocent, boyish look and an athleticism expressed through soccer and basketball. He is a top bridge player and an avid reader of Camus, Faulkner, and Steinbeck.

Étienne-Émile Baulieu is almost unique among scientists—brilliant, certainly, as his election to the French Academy of Sciences in 1983 attests, but just as skilled in promotion and public relations. Professor Lieberman praises his "extraordinary intelligence, his comprehensive knowledge, and his enormous scientific productivity." Dr. George Chrousos of the U.S. National Institutes of Health (NIH) rates him as a "very original scientist." Professor Jean Bernard, president of the French Academy, concludes that "he can't not be first" and cites his "tensions" and "his love of research which sustains them." In 1989 he won the Albert Lasker Clinical Medical Research Award. Many scientists consider this a prelude to the Nobel Prize.

Before election to the French Academy, Baulieu had identified brain cells that produce steroids. He had discovered that adrenal glands secrete a steroid soluble in water, broadening our grasp of how that hormone is transported in the blood supply. But it is RU 486 that has turned Baulieu into a public eminence—the "world's most controversial scientist," the Columbus, Ohio, *Dispatch* called him.

One element of his public relations success is his high-placed contacts. "Baulieu could get an appointment with the president of France without much trouble, while I'd have a lot of difficulty," Sakiz points out. A U.S. family planning executive, trying to locate Baulieu, finally tracked him down in Palm Springs, California, at the home of Walter Annenberg, a former U.S. ambassador to Britain and owner of one of the country's best private art collections. He often stays in Washington with the French ambassador, and after a late afternoon interview at his Paris laboratory recently, he rushed off to put on a black tie for a dinner party for the U.S. ambassador to France. "He's a political animal with political clout," concludes Dr. Kathryn Horwitz of the University of Colorado Health Sciences Center.

Virtually commuting to the United States in recent years for public rallies and TV appearances on RU 486, Baulieu has been labeled a "one-man show" by an NIH scientist. He is adroit at handling the press. Sakiz considers him "charming and elegant," but Dr. André Ulmann, a Roussel executive, says he can "often act like a spoiled child." Angier Biddle Duke, the former U.S. ambassador to Spain, calls him an "Olympian figure, an Adlai Stevenson type. He can talk on anything."

He combines many of the attributes of a Renaissance

man. He extols physical ability, skiing constantly. Although he has broken a leg three times, he boasts that "I passed one of the highest ski exams with a plaster cast on my leg." When he can't ski, he sails, mainly around Brittany. "Both are an obsession with me."

One of Baulieu's important Renaissance qualities, according to Professor Lieberman, is his "artistic feeling, his bohemianism." Sailing to New York on the *Liberté* in 1961, he met Barbara Rose, the art critic, soon to marry Frank Stella, and Clarissa Rivers, the wife of Larry Rivers. Through these men, both prominent artists, he quickly plunged into a circle of New York artists that included Jasper Johns and Robert Rauschenberg. He has since become a dedicated museum-goer, but oddly, collects no art. "I collect postcards," he insists puckishly. His humor is low-key. When Robin Duke, a former president of the National Abortion Rights Action League and a prominent hostess, had buttons made up that announced "Buy France: RU 486," Baulieu ordered hundreds and made everyone at the INSERM laboratories wear them.

Some observers consider Baulieu "irresistible" to women, and his relationship with Sophia Loren has been pretty well established. His face has grown slightly fleshy, but his hair shows only a hint of gray, and his skin remains unlined. His marriage to a dentist has produced three children—one daughter, a lawyer; another, a psychiatrist; and a son who is a physicist.

"Baulieu's office," remarks Dr. Paul Robel, a longtime associate, "resembles a Barnum circus." His desk is stacked with books and papers. His clothes are rumpled. He gives the impression of disorientation, yet he always seems to find the document he wants or calls the exact instruction to an aide. "An enlightened despot" is the way Professor Bernard describes him. "Impatient by character but patient by intelligence. He is smiling but anxious. Anxious about not doing enough. Anguished by the decisions to take."

Baulieu insists, "I know how to do things rapidly. I can see a museum in an hour. I always leave a dinner party by 11 P.M. I know what people have to say by then."

Baulieu was born in 1926 in France. His mother came from an old Norman family. His father was Léon Blum, a Jewish doctor in Strasbourg but unrelated to the former prime minister of the same name. They married when he was fifty and she thirty, a second marriage for him that was never approved by his wife's family. Dr. Blum was noted as one of the first physicians to introduce insulin into France and for treating the king of Egypt. "I was conceived in Egypt," Baulieu says.

When Baulieu was three years old, his father died, leaving three children. "I adored my mother," Baulieu says. "She was very beautiful." A lawyer with a master's degree in English, she was a dedicated suffragette who went to England often to join the demonstrations. She was a skilled pianist, and made piano lessons part of Baulieu's education. She lived to the age of ninety, and he still occupies the Paris apartment that she owned.

Although Baulieu could now be described as heavy-set, he says he was thin and weak as a child. In school he was first in every subject but got a zero in gym classes. His mother, who pushed him into skiing, also made him take private bodybuilding exercises. The next year he won first prize in gym.

After the Nazis invaded France, the family moved to Grenoble, which was still in the free zone, and changed their name from Blum to Baulieu to protect themselves from the increasing roundup of Jews and deportation to concentration camps. They got their new identity cards at Arras since the city hall and all its records had just burned down and anyone needing a new card could conveniently register there.

At the age of sixteen, while still in school, Baulieu joined the Maquis, or French underground. "We transported guns, obstructed railroad tracks to block the deportation of workers to Germany, and distributed Free French tracts," he recalls. Working with many young Communists, he saw them as the main force in rebuilding France and joined the party after Liberation. When the Soviet Union invaded Hungary in 1956, he resigned his membership.

This affiliation would come back to haunt him. He took his medical degree and doctorate in science after the war at the Faculté de Médicine in Paris. But when he later applied for a U.S. visa to study with Professor Lieberman in New York, the State Department turned him down. It was not until the more liberal administration of President John F. Kennedy came to power in 1961 and top administrators at Columbia University exerted pressure that he was finally allowed to enter the United States. "Baulieu always seemed angry in those days," remembers Pontus Hulten, an old friend and art historian. "Now he's far more patient."

At the age of twenty-nine, Baulieu became France's youngest professor of chemistry at the University of Rhiems, known as the "turbo professor" since he commuted from Paris once a week on high-speed turbo trains for six or seven hours of teaching. Dr. Pincus, who had pushed Baulieu into contraceptive research, had him placed on the World Health Organization's committee on contraception, which required further shuttling between Paris and Geneva. In 1965, Président Charles De Gaulle appointed Baulieu to the government's committee on contraception, which approved the birth control pill for nationwide use.

"No one was doing molecular biology in those days," Baulieu recalls. "I was working on steroid synthesis and sex hormones. I wanted to know how the receptor worked." His first published papers were received coldly, but he says, "I was confident that an anti-progestin could block the receptor."

The sharp differences that would soon erupt as to who was responsible for discovering RU 486 are hardly new in the scientific community. In 1990, for example, teams of U.S. and French scientists were still engaged in public debate over who had discovered the AIDS virus. But RU 486 was a special case. Not only did it involve a consultant and a research group in the same company, but Roussel had obviously decided on a public relations strategy to promote the pill and was using Baulieu as its instrument. At least three years before Dr. Teutsch and his group tried to clarify their contribution publicly, Baulieu had already become lionized as the pill's "discoverer."

The conflict inside Roussel broke out into the open on September 22, 1989, when Teutsch rebuked *Science* magazine for its article dating testing of the pill to 1978. "RU 486 was synthesized in April 1980," Teutsch asserted.

He further challenged the accuracy of the article, insisting that the story of "how RU 486 was designed does not fit the facts as I recall them as a member of the Roussel research team which was fully responsible for this discovery."

In an even sharper letter dated February 9, 1990, Teutsch, joined by Philibert, wrote that he "resented the recent and for the first time clearly stated claims about the design of RU 486."

Although he granted Baulieu the leading role in testing the pill, Teutsch insisted that "Raynaud and Philibert were responsible for receptor screening, not Baulieu. I found that steroidal epoxide could be used for a new compound, and about January or February 1975, we modified it at the eleventh position. We were the first. We discussed it for abortion, but Roussel wasn't ready for it."

On the other hand, Dr. Roger Deraedt, Roussel's director of health development, points out that "we thought it would be difficult to convince Roussel" and stresses that "Baulieu's influence on Sakiz was important."

Baulieu, in his version, insists that Teutsch's group thought that RU 486 was an agonist (imitating the hormone) while Roussel was searching for antagonists (inhibiting the hormone), and that without his pressure on top management, the new compound would have been ignored. Baulieu points out further that the group's research might have been stopped when RU 486 caused death in two out of three monkeys in toxicity tests, if he had not told management that death was a logical effect of prolonged treatment with potent doses of an anti-glucocorticoid. Since Baulieu's advice to Sakiz and other executives was verbal, no written record exists as to the impact of his advice and whether it affected continuation of Teutsch's research.

Determined to keep peace between these stellar scientists, Sakiz has worked hard at mediation. It would be "unfair," he concludes, to credit Baulieu with being the "father" of the pill when the patent and most research data on development come from Teutsch's group. Instead he calls Baulieu its "inspiration." He acknowledges that Baulieu "pushed us into the anti-hormone field. The speed of this accomplishment was due to him." He praises Baulieu's courage—"He dares to say what he thinks"—and his "brilliant public relations," which have been of "tremendous value to the company." Baulieu, in turn, claims that he has "produced millions of dollars in publicity for Roussel" and gets no royalties from the sale of RU 486.

A political factor made Baulieu's public relations role particularly important in 1982. With the election of François Mitterand as France's president and the government's purchase of a large stake in Roussel, Sakiz had to deal with the health ministry's attitude toward RU 486. The company was boxed in by Hoechst, its majority shareholder. Not only was its president, Wolfgang Hilger, a devout Roman Catholic and opposed to abortion, but Hoechst was the successor company to I. G. Farben, which had produced the gas for Hitler's concentration camp death-chambers. Hilger feared the "death pill" tag that opponents were already giving RU 486.

Hilger was additionally concerned by American opposition. One-fourth of Hoechst's $23 billion annual sales were made in the United States, and Catholic-Fundamentalist leaders had threatened to picket all the company's products.

When Roussel, therefore, submitted RU 486 to the health ministry for approval after thousands of successful tests in France, Britain, Scandinavia, and other countries, Baulieu's far-reaching campaign had already been instrumental in rousing public enthusiasm for the pill. On September 23, 1988, the French government announced to considerable fanfare that the pill would become publicly available through a network of hospitals and clinics, requiring that it be controlled by medical supervision and that the three-step process take place on medical premises.

In a furious reaction on TV, in the newspapers, and from the pulpit, Cardinal Jean-Marie Lustiger of Paris and other bishops condemned RU 486 as "savage liberalism" and a "chemical weapon" against the unborn. The church organized a march through Paris, but drew two thousand people at most. The health ministry and Roussel headquarters were picketed, and holders of a few shares of Roussel stock tried to interrupt the company's annual meeting. Catholic doctors wrote an estimated three hundred letters to the company threatening to boycott all Roussel products.

Although the opposition campaign had hardly stirred massive protests, Roussel announced on October 26 that it was taking the pill off the market. "We didn't want to get into a moral debate," explained Arlette Geslin, director of medical relations. The managing committee had voted 3 (including Sakiz) to 2 for this retreat. Given the strength of the company's commitment to Baulieu's public relations buildup, Roussel's fears seemed puzzling. They could be attributed to orders from Wolfgang Hilger, but Sakiz later insisted, "We have full independence from Hoechst." Sakiz would eventually claim that this retreat was a tactic to buy time for Claude Evin, the health minister, to harness support from political parties.

On the very day that Roussel pulled the pill, thousands of obstetricians and gynecologists were meeting at a world congress in Rio de Janeiro. Announcement of Roussel's retreat stunned the audience, and petitions were immediately drawn up and signed by most doctors, demanding that the health ministry reverse Roussel's decision. Dr. Annie Bureau, a Paris doctor, protested, "It denies women the benefits of scientific progress." Courageously attacking his own company, Baulieu told the meeting that Roussel's retreat was "morally scandalous."

A tragic incident in Paris also defused the Catholic campaign. Martin Scorsese's movie, *The Last Temptation of Christ*, had just opened at a Paris theater, and Catholics who considered it blasphemous kept picket lines around the entry. Someone threw a bomb into the theater, setting a fire that hospitalized thirteen people, one in critical condition. There was an immediate outburst of public anger against such consequences of fanaticism, which also bolstered opposition to a Catholic boycott of the pill. The governing Socialists, as well as almost all of France's political parties, rallied behind RU 486 and urged that it be restored to the health system.

In a ringing statement on October 28, 1988, declaring his decision was made "out of concern for the public health and what this pill means for women," health minister Evin ordered it back on the market. According to a 1968 law, he had considerable power over Roussel.

Not only did the government own 36 percent of the company, but it could remove the company's license and award it to another manufacturer if a drug that had been proven safe and effective was withdrawn from public use.

Catholic opposition dwindled away. "We had a local priest who used to come to my hospital, demanding that I stop administering RU 486," explains Dr. Elizabeth Aubeny of Broussais Hospital in Paris. "I would point to a sign on the wall, stating something like 'If you want to keep your pregnancy, take the following steps.' He liked that sign. Now he comes back often to check that it's still there, but never protests the pill. We have a 'gentleman's agreement.' We're at peace now."

4

Women and Their Reactions

In a clinic at the massive Broussais Hospital in Paris, twenty-four-year-old Carine C. swallowed a small tablet of RU 486 with a glass of water and exulted, "It's almost magic. Almost magic but not quite."

Marie-Pierre S., a twenty-eight-year-old restaurateur with one child, chose RU 486 as a "more natural" method of abortion. "I didn't want to be in a medical atmosphere, like it was an illness or disease." A thirty-one-year-old decorator with one child, preferred "no surgery aggression."

At Maternité des Lilas, a clinic in the Paris suburbs where babies are delivered and abortions are performed, other women stressed the psychological advantages of the pill. "I felt as if I was having a miscarriage, me, on my own, almost naturally," one reported. "It was different from a normal abortion where someone removes the egg from you." Florence D., a thirty-year-old mother of two, insisted, "It's less traumatic . . . you are aware and conscious of what's happening." Twenty-eight-year-old Camille A. concluded, "There is no intrusion on the integrity of the body." A twenty-five-year-old single student called the pill "gentle, safe, and sane."

Dr. David Grimes at the University of Southern California in Los Angeles has run successful tests—the only abortion tests that Roussel has allowed in the United States—on almost four hundred women. Of this group, Kyle X., a married woman who had delivered twins in October 1988, found herself pregnant again in September 1989 due to contraceptive failure. "I was too exhausted to have another child immediately," she recalls. "I heard about RU 486 through friends. I wasn't worried about bleeding—I had faith in my body. I took the pill on a Tuesday and started spotting a little. I had the prostaglandin shot on Friday and rested about forty-five minutes. There was only mild cramping and nausea. My husband drove me home. It was just heavy bleeding for three days like a miscarriage, tapering off in a week or so. I couldn't see any tissue or solid matter. What I liked was taking care of myself, not being in the hands of doctors. It brought a sense of knowledge and control, a positive existential experience."

After tabulating a thousand RU 486 cases at the Broussais Hospital, Dr. Elisabeth Aubeny found from her first seventy-five interviews that almost 100 percent were "satisfied with their choice." All emphasize the responsibility they have decided to take," she points out. "Instead of being passive as they are in vacuum aspiration, they manage their own abortions. By taking the tablet, the woman acts to trigger the process and supervises evacuation at home. In the vacuum technique, a doctor is in sole control. A woman can be virtually absent if she chooses general anesthesia. But RU 486 fits the needs of responsible patients who can cope by themselves, as many women want to do."

By 1990, almost a third of French women wanting

abortion and less than nine weeks pregnant had picked RU 486 over vacuum abortion once both techniques were explained to them. Doctors report that the number of women choosing RU 486 is rising as women describe its advantages to others.

By creating a focus for personal responsibility, RU 486 has gained widespread support from feminist groups. Recognizing that taking a pill is less invasive than surgery, many women are convinced that RU 486 has freed them from institutional constraints, that it has humanized and "de-medicalized" abortion. It has transformed women's experience, a decisive step that forced "me to grow up," as one woman put it. "A new thought process has been started, which adds an extra dimension to women's history," concludes Chantal Birman, a midwife for eighteen years who works at the Lilas Clinic.

Women who prefer vacuum abortion, particularly professionals with tight schedules, "want everything done quickly and in one step," Dr. Aubeny explains. One patient felt "constant anguish" over seeing her bleeding. "You see everything that takes place and that's difficult," complained another. "I would have preferred the doctor to have taken complete charge of everything," one woman told Dr. Aubeny.

It must always be recognized that the decision to have an abortion is one of the most tortured steps a woman will ever take. No woman ever wants an abortion, but almost all women realize its necessity at a critical time. Not only is a woman temporarily blocking her procreative function, but she is submitting her body to the control of an outside party, a doctor usually unknown to her. A teenager, in particular, not only may face a traumatic experience, but if her parents, husband, or partner offer no support, may be facing it alone.

Although the basic instinct of a woman is to go on with a pregnancy, she may be so overwhelmed by economic, social, family health, and other pressures that an abortion is the only way to maintain her well-being and stability. It is an agonizing choice no matter how strong the needs impelling it.

With such attendant stresses, the advantages of RU 486 are significant. In addition to eliminating the bodily invasion of vacuum abortion, RU 486 helps a woman feel that she is far more than flesh on a table subject to medical routine. It guarantees the sensitivity of a patient and makes her master of her life. Above all, it ensures her dignity.

Although opponents have insisted that RU 486 has made abortions easier and will invariably increase their number, French statistics show exactly the opposite result. Abortions have hardly risen since 1982, when the French social security system started covering most of the cost. In 1986, there were 166,797 abortions, according to the ministry of health. In 1988, after RU 486 was approved for national use, there were 162,598. Since French law allows abortion only in the first twelve weeks of pregnancy, experts estimate that about four thousand annually go to Britain or the Netherlands for abortion in the later stages of pregnancy.

The numerical stability of French abortions among teenagers, generally duplicated throughout Western Europe, is in glaring contrast with the trend in the United States. Pregnancies per 1,000 unmarried girls fifteen to nineteen years of age in a recent study were 96 in the

United States, 45 in England and Wales, and 14 in the Netherlands. This low and stable rate of abortion stems from three factors critical to the European record. First, contraception is free or sold at minimum cost and available at a broad range of public and private agencies. Second, contraceptive information is easily accessible to everyone, including teenagers. In Britain, for example, pharmacies serve as centers for birth control education. Finally, sex education has been made part of the school curriculum in many European countries, and often it is mandatory.

A significant advantage of RU 486 is that it encourages women, particularly the young, to confront their pregnancies and act quickly if they decide on abortion. Complications before nine weeks with RU 486 have been rare. Of the first fifty thousand cases in France, the two complications involved women thirty-five and thirty-eight years old, one a heavy smoker, the other under severe psychological stress. Both women recovered completely. Doctors believe these complications were due to prostaglandin, and they now avoid giving the pill to older patients who have a predisposition to cardiovascular risks.

By contrast, without disparaging the method on which U.S. women have had to rely, vacuum abortion has a complication rate of 4 to 6 percent if done in the first six weeks, when the embryo is small and often missed. Hospitals and clinics, therefore, generally urge women to postpone a vacuum abortion until after eight weeks of pregnancy.

The principal annoyances women experience from RU 486 combined with prostaglandin are uterine contractions, light nausea, and diarrhea, which are due to the administration of prostaglandin and may continue for a few hours. "Most women have no pain at all," Dr. Elisabeth Aubeny explains. In a multinational study of 251 women done by the World Health Organization, only 7.6 percent had enough pain to require narcotic analgesics. In a British study of about 1,000 cases, Dr. Ian Z. Mackenzie, a leading researcher at John Radcliffe Hospital in Oxford, reported that 48 percent had no pain, 29 percent had enough discomfort for aspirin, and 23 percent needed a painkiller.

Pain seems to depend somewhat on the strength of the dosage of two different types of prostaglandin, sulprostone and gemeprost, which are chemically different but act the same. In a 1990 study of 2,115 French women, pain was more intense in those who received high and intermediate doses of sulprostone. Although expulsion was more rapid in those who received the high dose of sulprostone, uterine bleeding decreased in those who received the low dose of both sulprostone and gemeprost. Researchers have no adequate explanation yet for this last finding.

Another concern raised about the use of RU 486 is the three-step process and the possibility that some women may drop out before completing it. No evidence in France or Britain supports this concern. Dr. Danielle Gaudry and Dr. Sadan Ouri, a husband-wife team at a Paris hospital serving many poor Africans, insist, "We have had no problem with the poor and uneducated when we explain things in their language and stress their responsibility. All our women have come back." In a study of 353 women at the Broussais Hospital in Paris, Dr. Annie Bureau reported that "none of the women was lost to follow-up." Dr. Mackenzie says of the British trials, "I'm not concerned about women coming back. The record here so far supports that."

The French system, of course, has built-in features that augment responsibility. Under French law, passed provisionally in January 1975 and finally in December 1979, all abortions must be performed in hospitals and clinics. Women must have French nationality or have lived in the country for three months. Their addresses, phone numbers, and social security numbers (if any) are checked. On the first visit, a woman is told the details of both vacuum and RU 486 abortion. Her length of pregnancy is determined by gynecological examination. The pill must be administered within forty-nine days of the last period if she wants an RU 486 abortion. Plasma levels and blood tests are taken if the doctor thinks they're necessary.

On the second visit a week later, the woman signs a form agreeing to abortion, as required by law. The doctor checks whether any further tests are necessary, and then she is given the RU 486 pill.

On the third visit a day or two later, the woman takes a dose of prostaglandin—the French prefer injection to vaginal application. She remains at the hospital or clinic resting for three or four hours after the injection. Sedatives are given in case of pain. Expulsion usually takes place in three hours or less.

On the fourth visit a week or so later, a medical exam confirms that abortion has been completed successfully and the bleeding has stopped. A social worker questions the woman as to her physical and psychological reactions. In those rare cases when RU 486 has failed, a vacuum abortion is recommended.

After long negotiations with Roussel, the French government set a price of about $256 for one dose of RU 486, the prostaglandin, and medical checkups. The cost of vacuum abortion is about $247. In both cases, 80 percent of the cost is refunded to the woman by the social security system.

As dedicated proponents of the Mouvement Français pour le Planning Familial, which corresponds to the Planned Parenthood Federation of America, Dr. Gaudry and Dr. Ouri want the women's movement to have more responsibility in administering RU 486 and vacuum abortion. With headquarters in Paris, the Mouvement has twenty-three regional federations and ninety departmental associations, and joined the International Planned Parenthood Federation in 1959. It presently only advises on contraception and abortion and refers women to hospitals and clinics. It also takes an aggressive political stance on such issues as incest, rape, family violence, and sexual violence against children. But despite having a medical staff, the Mouvement is not permitted by French law to perform abortions at its Paris headquarters or other offices.

The problem is not women's privacy, as it has become in the United States with picketing, invasion, and destruction of clinics. The French system, requiring hospitals and clinic abortion in settings where childbirth and other gynecological procedures are also performed, provides an anonymous environment for an abortion patient. The problem is shifting more authority to women's groups and feminists. "We want more control in women's hands. Abortion could be done at family planning clinics," Gaudry and Ouri insist.

The same issue may come up in Britain, where most

abortions take place in hospitals administered under the National Health Service (NHS). Although Roussel did not make application for a product license for RU 486 until 1990, the Birth Control Trust, a private organization that advises members of Parliament on all aspects of family planning, prepared the public the year before with a highly publicized meeting of experts. A 1987 poll showed that 79 percent of the country supported abortion on request.

Still, British law has peculiar limitations. Allowing abortion up to twenty-four weeks (contrasted with twelve weeks in France), it requires approval on physical or mental health grounds by two doctors (contrasted with abortion on demand in France). Britain requires by law that abortion be done in hospitals or clinics approved by the government. Medical tradition usually requires general anesthesia. This means that practically all patients must stay overnight. Almost half of abortions are done free under the NHS. The rest are done for a nominal charge.

This system has been interpreted liberally by Marie Stopes International, a privately owned organization with three hospitals in London and many clinics in India, Indonesia, Sierra Leone, and other African nations. It does twenty-two thousand abortions annually in London at a sliding scale of up to $345. When a doctor remains on duty and the patient lives near one of its hospitals, Stopes sends patients home after abortion as frequently as 45 percent of the time.

"We should follow the same procedure with RU 486," declares Dr. Timothy R. L. Black, Stopes's chief executive. "We want to put as much responsibility in the woman's hands as possible."

The approval process for RU 486 in Britain goes through

the Committee on Safety of Medicine, a governmental group that has the final say on drugs and medications. Dr. David Paintin, an obstetrician-gynecologist at St. Mary's Hospital Medical School in London and an officer of the Birth Control Trust, feels confident that the committee will accept the data from fifty thousand French cases as well as about one thousand tests in Britain.

Dr. Mackenzie has tabulated a monetary advantage in the use of RU 486. Since the cost of an RU 486 abortion will run about seventy-five dollars, it will save the British government about half of the current cost when performed without hospitalization. Anesthesia, surgeon fees, and overnight hospitalization fees will be eliminated.

Still, the pressure on the government from a highly organized minority opposition has provoked sharp parliamentary debate. In two previous attempts in Parliament to cut the number of weeks during which abortion was allowed, the opposition sometimes gathered as many as 250 votes out of about 550 voting. This reflects an overweighted influence at the local level from hard-core conservatives. "The government has been weak on family planning, sex education, and related issues, leaving them under control of local governing bodies, where conservatives throw their weight around," explains Dilys Cossey, head of the British Family Planning Association.

The opposition stems from the Society for the Protection of the Unborn Child, made up of conservative Catholics and such Fundamentalists as the Plymouth Brethren. But even the Church of England, Baptists, and Methodists contain evangelical factions. A new fanaticism has been added by the arrival of organizers from the United States, who have started to picket and block clinic entrances, adopting the tactics of Operation Rescue.

British research has recently expanded the use of RU 486 beyond early abortion and enhanced its advantages for women. British law allows abortion in the period of thirteen to eighteen weeks of pregnancy known as "midterm," and 29,000 out of a total of 183,000 abortions in 1988 were performed then. The sole therapy previously consisted of a dose of prostaglandin, which induces uterine contractions and helps expel the fetus. But the drawbacks were the heavy side effects and lengthy time needed for fetal expulsion.

In 1987, consequently, Dr. Mackenzie and his associates experimented with giving a prior dose of RU 486 as a "priming procedure." After thousands of tests, they reported that the trials were "effective" and provided a "more exciting new approach." By giving RU 486 first, the procedure now requires less prostaglandin, thus reducing side effects such as nausea and diminishing abortion time. In fact, the combination of the two drugs often cuts the usual 15-hours for mid-term abortions in half, and means that some patients can now be kept on the ward just for only one day rather than being confined overnight.

Few other countries have analyzed women's physical and emotional reactions. Because of its critical need for population control, China began testing RU 486 soon after France and ran multicenter trials on two thousand women. "About 80 percent of the women preferred the medical interruption to vacuum aspiration," reports Dr. Gao-Ji of the National Research Institute for Family Planning. "The main advantages of the method are considered by the acceptors to be less pain, quicker recovery, and less psychological pressure compared with surgery." Although early trials used RU 486 supplied by Roussel, Chinese researchers have since synthesized their own version of RU 486, which is now undergoing clinical trials in Shanghai.

In Sweden, where RU 486 is expected to be approved for public use in 1991, a study in 1984 showed a strong demand for medical abortion at home when prostaglandin was being given alone. Dr. A. S. Rosen of the University of Stockholm, Dr. Marc Bygdeman of Karolinska Hospital, and their associates performed early abortion on 53 women—17 at home and 18 in the hospital with prostaglandin, 18 in the hospital with vacuum aspiration.

During interviews with social workers beforehand, two-thirds of the women stated they preferred medical abortion at home. "They frequently mentioned that they would feel more at ease and more secure in their usual milieu," the study found. "Several women said that their husbands would stay at home with them, and/or that the abortion not only concerned the woman but also her partner, who should give his help and support during the treatment."

After the abortion, the women were interviewed again. "The home treatment group rated their own abortion procedure as significantly more harmless (versus frightening) after abortion than when first interviewed," the study concluded. Although this research was done before scientists discovered the advantage of giving RU 486 before prostaglandin, and although prostaglandin administered alone has more side effects than the combined treatment, the results emphasized the "pronounced positive attitude towards the home abortion procedure present in the entire group before treatment."

It is home treatment, of course, that will guarantee women the ultimate in privacy. And it is privacy, particularly in the United States, that makes RU 486 a boon to women.

5

World Distribution of RU 486: The Role of Elitism

The worldwide distribution of RU 486 represents a problem of elitism. The nations selected by the Roussel Company in 1990 to be the next recipients after France of this critical drug have gained priority not because of greater need but because of convenience. Great Britain, Holland, and Scandinavia were apparently chosen on the grounds that they were predominantly Protestant, that they had high medical standards and a controlled delivery system, and that the possibility of right-to-life opposition and national controversy leading to a boycott of Roussel products was minimal.

The underdeveloped countries, by contrast, despite their acute shortage of safe and accessible abortion, have not even been considered as sites for RU 486. Despite the World Health Organization's estimate that 200,000 women a year in Africa, Asia, and other underdeveloped areas die from botched abortions at the hands of illegal clinics and quacks, few international organizations except for WHO and the Population Council have called attention to this disaster or made it a matter of international priority. No one has tried to count the number of women whose health or reproductive capacity has been ruined.

The rationale for bypassing the developing world is that the chance of hemorrhage after the prostaglandin dose demands close follow-up care by doctors or nurse practitioners in hospitals and clinics, which may be difficult, if not impossible, in most underdeveloped countries. But the incidence of hemorrhage has been almost negligible in fifty thousand French women and thousands of others upon whom the drug has been tested in Britain and elsewhere. The problem, therefore, must be put into perspective. While no woman, poor or rich, should chance a medical risk, the slight possibility of hemorrhage must be weighed against hundreds of thousands of certain deaths. There is a reasonable alternative to ignoring the underdeveloped world. Many countries where abortion is legal could develop a network of skilled medical technicians, who would not only be trained in the administration of RU 486, but who would have backup and medical facilities available within a practical distance in case of emergency.

The need for this and other alternative approaches becomes more pressing in the context of rapidly expanding populations. The United Nations Fund for Population Activities estimates that the present world population of 5.3 billion will soar to 6.25 billion by the end of this century, with the populations of poorer nations accounting for up to 80 percent of this total. Nearly one billion people already live in poverty. Overpopulation and poverty can never be solved by abortion. Further, the choice of abortion must always come from the woman herself, but the pressure created by poverty in underdeveloped nations undoubtedly intensifies the frequency and desperation of this choice.

In Bangladesh, for example, a country the size of Wisconsin but with a population of 107 million, "unemployment or underemployment already affect 50 percent of the labor force," according to a report issued by the International Women's Health Coalition. "It is hard to envision how jobs can be found for the additional one million people entering the labor force each year."

Poverty ranks as a major factor in forcing an estimated 800,000 Bangladeshi women each year to resort to abortion by "untrained quacks." The Health Coalition cites the case of Zarina, who, at age thirty-three, had already borne eight children, six of whom survived: "Desperate to avoid another birth, Zarina recently turned to the local, traditional midwife for abortion. She hemorrhaged and nearly died; now she is unable to perform the hard labor required for her own and her family's sustenance."

Although cases like Zarina are common in Bangladesh, the government has tried to meet the emergency by developing a network of medical technicians who perform menstrual regulation (MR) and who could eventually be taught to administer RU 486. Its safety and simplicity of administration make the pill a potential boon to Bangladeshi women. A supervised trial of RU 486 should be conducted immediately in collaboration with the World Health Organization. Health and Family Welfare Centers throughout Bangladesh have long been staffed by 3,300 women technicians trained in an eighteen-month-long course. They counsel women on reproductive health and contraception. Known as Family Welfare Visitors, they take an additional six-week-long course to specialize in MR. In fact, these female paramedics perform far more MR's than doctors, who have also been trained in it. Mostly men, these doctors are rarely welcomed by the typically modest Bangladeshi women.

Menstrual regulation could be construed as abortion, but the Islamic religion does not consider early intervention an abortion. Instead, MR is described as "washing out the uterus." Officially supported by the government since 1975, MR involves the "induction of shedding the endometrium or lining of the uterus before or shortly after the expected day of onset of menstruation, if an unwanted conception is suspected," Professor Syeda Firoza Begum of Bangladesh explains. Rather than mentioning a possible fetus, the government emphasizes restoration of menstruation, MR's objective being "to clean the uterine lining of any obstruction to menstruation."

MR supposedly must be done within two weeks after a woman has missed her menstrual period. But this limit can be stretched to six or eight weeks. The process is fairly simple. The Family Welfare Visitor uses a bulb syringe (with single or double valve) attached to a flexible cannula, which is inserted into the womb. When the plunger is pulled out, creating a vacuum, the pressure is strong enough to cleanse the uterine lining of a developing embryo.

A few clinics are also equipped with a suction machine and hand pump, which aspirate the uterus through the same process as the vacuum abortion technique of industrialized nations. The use of electric-powered aspiration, however, is still uncommon in Bangladesh.

The syringe in the hands of a trained paramedic has proved remarkably effective, accounting for almost all of the eight-five thousand MR's recorded each year, at a cost of about six dollars each. This total is considered low since many procedures are performed at the homes of paramedics and doctors, who make extra money on the side and never report it.

Private groups are reaching more rural areas. The Bangladesh Women's Health Coalition has seven clinics and plans to add more, doing at least five hundred MR's a month. It concentrates not just on family planning and women's health care in general, but has become a political force on all women's issues.

Possibly the most significant aspect of this system is the high level of safety and efficiency achieved by women paramedics in comparison with physicians. One study shows that only 15 percent of the patients of Family Welfare Visitors, compared with nearly 17 percent of the doctors' patients, "had some complications after receiving MR services."

Considering the ability of Bangladesh to train skilled paramedics, why should similar personnel not be trained in the administration of RU 486? Admittedly, there are problems. Poor rural transportation, involving rivers more often than roads, would make it more difficult for Bangladeshi women to complete the multistep process required by RU 486. This means that the first tests would have to be confined to Dhaka and other large cities, and that the combination of RU 486 and prostaglandin in one pill or injection would make the process far more efficient.

Since any drug can be purchased in Bangladesh without a prescription, tighter controls on RU 486 and other drugs would have to be legislated. Another obstacle is that women have so many children and their periods are so irregular that few can accurately confirm their pregnancies. Paramedics would have to be taught this expertise. A woman taking a black-market pill without medical supervision of its consequences risks the possibility of bringing a damaged fetus to term, or of having dangerous bleeding or infection complicating an incomplete abortion.

There are political and cultural obstacles as well. Political extremists often oppose any innovation that leads to "Westernizing" or "experimenting on" Bangladeshi women. Still, Dr. Atiquer Rahman Khan, who directed the first MR clinic in 1975, insists that public acceptance could be hastened by calling the RU 486 process "medical menstrual regulation."

While these obstacles could delay a trial of RU 486 in Bangladesh or a similar underdeveloped country for years, recent advances that have improved the pill have significant implications for Europe and the United States as well as for poorer regions. One advance is the possibility of a low-dosage pill of 200 milligrams instead of the present 600 milligram dose that has been used in France. Similarly, the dose of prostaglandin may be radically reduced to 0.125 milligrams. These lower dosages not only would benefit women by diminishing such side effects as nausea, vomiting, and pain, but would especially benefit the poor by making abortion potentially less expensive than it now is in France.

In a World Health Organization multicenter trial in Britain in 1989, 250 women were given RU 486 in doses ranging from 150 to 200 milligrams with a success rate of 94 percent (one center was excluded when the outcome could not be adequately determined). Thereupon, WHO launched trials in twelve centers, including ones in China, Hungary, Hong Kong, Italy, Sweden, and Yugoslavia. From late 1989 to late 1990, 1,188 women were tested at the 200 milligram dosage. Even before the trials were completed, two leading experts predicted excellent results. "I wouldn't hesitate to bet that 200 milligrams would be completely effective," states Dr. Paul F. A. Van Look, who supervises the program for WHO. "There is no question in my mind that 200 milligrams or less is enough of a dose," confirms Dr. Jose Barzelatto, senior program adviser for the Ford Foundation and former director of the WHO program.

Although France still adheres to the 600 milligram dose set by early trials, British regulations do not set a dosage level for RU 486. Consequently, any hospital or clinic can switch to 200 milligrams at its discretion. "The whole world will be using the reduced dosage," concludes Barzelatto.

More important for women in underdeveloped countries, with problems of transportation and absence from their families and jobs during the multistep process, is the possibility of combining RU 486 and prostaglandin in one formulation. RU 486 takes at least thirty-six hours to act on the uterus. Combining prostaglandin with it in pill form would require a time-release mechanism. An intramuscular injection of both drugs, therefore, has become the more feasible objective of ongoing research.

In addition, a combined dosage presents patent problems. Since the Schering Company of West Germany not only makes prostaglandin, but also controls the patent on the structure and process of combining prostaglandin with an anti-progestin, the Roussel Company has been negotiating with Schering to work out an arrangement that would result in a combined dosage. Roussel also has access to a prostaglandin made by Rhone Poulenc, a nationalized French company. Another possibility is that a prostaglandin developed by Dr. Sune Bergstrom, former rector of Sweden's Karolinska Hospital, could be acquired by Roussel. With all these alternatives, it would be tragic indeed for patent squabbles and the rivalry between drug manufacturers to hold up medical progress that could benefit so many women, particularly the poor.

Even the introduction of RU 486 into Britain and Europe has suffered from administrative delays. It was late in 1990 before Roussel applied for a product license as required by British law. Parliament debated until June 21, 1990, before passing new legislation that extends the powers of the secretary of state for health to facilitate administration of RU 486 by general practitioners. British medicine had always used RU 486 in its tests through nine weeks of pregnancy (two weeks longer than France), and the new law does not restrict this time period. Although British medical practice usually performed vacuum abortion under general anesthesia with an overnight stay, the new law omits such requirements for any type of abortion. While the time limit for abortion was lowered from twenty-eight to twenty-four weeks of pregnancy, this new cutoff date presents no problem because twenty-four weeks was always observed by doctors. Thus the new limit had no significance except that congenital defects diagnosed after twenty-four weeks now had to be considered for special treatment.

The most disturbing aspect of RU 486's distribution in Europe was Roussel's decision to exclude West Germany. This decision could stem from the fact that Wolfgang Hilger, president of Hoechst, Roussel's parent company and a devout Catholic, objected to German distribution. More likely, it may be linked to the politics of the ruling Christian Democratic party and its relationship with the Vatican and the German Catholic hierarchy. In a nation almost evenly split between Catholics and Protestants, West Germany allows women access to abortion, but only under restricted conditions. Two doctors must approve an application, and a woman must consult a registered counselor. Approval may be given for an abortion through the twelfth week of pregnancy for rape, or if the pregnancy causes a woman great physical or emotional distress. It may be given through the twenty-second week for severe genetic damage to the fetus, or at any time for an emergency involving the woman's health. These restrictions are often interpreted loosely in the Protestant north, but in the south, particularly in Catholic states like Bavaria, tighter controls force many women to seek help in the north, in the Netherlands or in nearby countries, or from an underground practitioner.

With the reunification of Germany, abortion has become "one of the most divisive issues between East and West Germany," according to the *New York Times*. A unified Germany must deal with 17 million mostly Protestant East Germans who have long enjoyed an unhindered right to no-cost abortion through the twelfth week of pregnancy. An opinion poll in 1990 by the East German government showed that 77 percent of its citizens wanted to maintain the current laws, 12 percent gave no opinion, and 11 percent favored West German laws. East Germany, with its population of 17 million, performed

73,000 abortions in 1989. West Germany, with 60 million people, performed 75,000. East Germany, of course, had limited access to contraception.

Working with the women's movement in West Germany, which wants abortion removed from Bonn's criminal code, the Independent Women's Alliance in East Berlin has organized a flood of abortion rights petitions with 100,000 signatures. Catholics in Bavaria, coordinating with religious groups in Dresden, have collected 20,000 opposition signatures. The conflict has become so tense that the health ministers of East and West Germany failed to reach an agreement after numerous meetings in the period before reunification in October 1990. "The gap between the two positions is clearly unbridgeable," declared a spokesman at the West German Justice Ministry.

The impasse raises the issue of economic security as well as that of women's rights. As a result of unification, many East German jobs are threatened, particularly those of women who cannot risk time off for childbearing and infant care. Knowing there will be a superfluity of nurses, Isolde Thielen, a thirty-two-year-old nurse, feared that if she had a baby, she could not work alternating hospital shifts. Sylvia Landau, a twenty-six-year-old lawyer, mother of a ten-month-old child, and a prosecutor for the City of East Berlin, worries that if she became pregnant, the imposition of West Germany's abortion law on the East "would be a terrible step backward for us."

In a last-minute compromise, East and West Germany agreed to keep the present laws in each area until 1992. It would be ludicrous, indeed, for Rumania to reverse its detested ban on abortion immediately after the overthrow of Nicolae Ceausescu, while a unified Germany dilutes the abortion rights that women had long enjoyed in the Communist East.

Poland's abortion politics have become even more aggravated than Germany's. With contraceptives always in short supply and condoms of poor quality, as in all East European countries, abortion has been the main technique of controlling childbearing under Communism. In a country where 90 percent of the people list themselves as Catholics, more than one-half (at least 600,000) of all pregnancies were terminated by abortion last year.

The rise of Solidarity and the fall of Communism, however, have restored the traditional power of the Catholic bishops and unleashed a religious and political anti-abortion tide. After legalization of the Catholic church in June 1989, a new anti-abortion law, drawn by lawyers from the Bishops conference, was introduced to the lower house of Parliament by seventy deputies, mainly from Solidarity's conservative bloc. A convicted woman could be punished with three years' imprisonment. This was followed in 1990 by a Senate bill, passed by 50 to 17, that would make abortion a criminal offense except when two doctors confirmed a high risk to the woman's life.

The nascent Polish women's movement was constantly outmaneuvered. None of its representatives was allowed to appear at a Senate Health Commission hearing on the bill, a hearing to which Catholic clergy and anti-abortion doctors were invited. Only one newspaper managed to get a copy of the bill and print it. When women's groups held a pro-choice demonstration in Poznan, they were physically assaulted by opposition crowds, including a deputy to Parliament from the Christian National Union.

Women, in fact, have been virtually excluded from leadership in the fledgling democracy. None heads any Solidarity district. They make up only 12 percent of Parliament. At the Second Congress of Solidarity in April 1990, a resolution supporting "legislative protection of unborn life" was passed by 248 votes to 71, with 57 abstentions. Women represented only a tenth of the delegates. As a result of the "domination of national-Catholic conservatives," and the rigorous intervention of the Vatican, Barbara Limanowska of the Polish Feminist Association has warned that an anti-abortion bill could be pushed through the Polish Parliament in 1991. Anne-Marie Rey, co-president of the Swiss Union for Decriminalization of Abortion, has forecast a "terrible irony of history, if the process of democratization and return of self-determination of the Polish people end up by depriving women of a fundamental right and an essential liberty."

Abortion, and the distribution of RU 486 specifically, have thus become the focus of an international struggle in which women so far are the victims. Corporate decisions have been stacked against human needs. Elitist medicine has taken precedence over women's access to a critical drug. In underdeveloped countries, the Roussel Company has ignored millions of women on the grounds that the slim possibility of hemorrhage from RU 486 without an immediate hospital backup could damage the corporate image of safety. Even though the risks are minimal, and could be largely controlled by a Bangladesh model of medical technicians, the plight of poor countries must be sacrificed to corporate fears that any divergence from conservative medicine could endanger profits.

Roussel's failure to distribute RU 486 in Poland, Germany, and other areas with pivotal Catholic influence reflects the company's avoidance of political controversy. A monopoly product brings a company the power to set its own rules. But by limiting distribution of a drug crucial to women even in industrialized nations, Roussel has established a precedent that could mean that any cure, whether for cancer or for AIDS, could be made available only at a manufacturer's whim.

The decision to keep RU 486 out of politically sensitive countries has produced a total denigration of women's rights. It will take the development of similar products— Schering's compounds, for example—to break this elitist grip. China, in fact, has synthesized its own brand of RU 486, and Roussel has not yet tried to stop ongoing tests. Other countries have developed anti-progestins that virtually duplicate the function of RU 486 but might be different enough to avoid a patent conflict. If science is to serve society and not just a corporation's narrow objectives, the women's movement must build the strength to guarantee that elitist medicine will never dominate feminist priorities.

Other Medical Uses
for RU 486

It is a remarkable testament to the versatility of RU 486 that this compound not only has been used for abortion in France and in other countries, but may well become an important contraceptive. Whether taken as a postcoital contraceptive or at the time women expect or have just missed their menses, it could eliminate the possibility of pregnancy, with women never knowing if they were pregnant or not. Another advantage is that as few as twelve doses a year may be the maximum required, in contrast to about 240 doses of the present birth control pills. The basic principle of RU 486's use as a contraceptive is that by inhibiting progesterone, it prevents preparation of the uterus for implantation of the egg.

Although contraceptive research has been held back due to the concentration on RU 486 as an abortifacient, Dr. Gary D. Hodgen, scientific director of the East Virginia Medical School at Norfolk, has already announced the compound's "effectiveness in inducing menstruation" and its potential "as a postcoital contraceptive." Dr. Lynette Nieman of the National Institutes of Health and her associates called RU 486 in 1987 a promising "form of fertility control that can be administered once a month" when "given three days before the desired day of menses." One study by Dr. Nieman reported that none of seventeen previously fertile monkeys, exposed to fertile males, became pregnant after receiving RU 486, while nine of thirty-three receiving placebos became pregnant.

Dr. Douglas R. Danforth's study in 1989 showed that RU 486 "blocks ovulation" and "during the luteal/secretory phase of the menstrual cycle induces premature menses in women and monkeys." Two other studies at that time found that "several different regimens of RU 486 can block ovulation in women" at very low doses.

Summarizing three trials, Dr. Paul F. A. Van Look of the World Health Organization reports a failure rate with RU 486 contraception of 8 women out of 199. This amounts to a failure rate of 4 percent per treated cycle. "In order to be effective as a 'once-a-month' contraceptive," Dr. Van Look believes that "RU 486 would probably have to be taken in combination with a prostaglandin analogue" so that each drug could strengthen the other's action.

Although this research is still experimental, Dr. Tina Agoestina of the University of Indonesia defines its scope: "RU 486 can be used as a 'medical menstrual regulator', or as a late 'postcoital' or late 'morning after' pill, i.e., as a contragestive." In sum, RU 486 acts as a contraceptive when taken between the fourteenth day and the twenty-eighth day of the menstrual cycle, which is normally twenty-eight days.

The most optimistic results so far have come from Dr. Samuel Yen of the University of California School of Medicine at San Diego. In phase one and phase two of his trials on women protected against pregnancy (using a diaphragm or other mechanical means of birth control), Yen's study in 1990, covering dosage, bleeding, and other reactions, rates RU 486 "very good" as a contraceptive. Now he has started on phase three, trials with women unprotected against pregnancy.

An important problem still to be solved involves the possibility of double bleeding. A woman taking RU 486 as a contraceptive would not only bleed at that time but possibly again at the time of her normal end-of-cycle. This could disorganize her monthly cycle. Although Dr. Yen "did not encounter" this problem in his trials, many women have irregular cycles ordinarily, and they might have trouble figuring out when they should take their dose of RU 486. The chances of double bleeding are greatly diminished by taking RU 486 two or three days before expected menses.

Dr. Marc Bygdeman of the Karolinska Hospital in Stockholm, who initiated the research on combining prostaglandin with RU 486, has become convinced that a single monthly dose of the compound can prevent pregnancy without the woman ever knowing whether or not fertilization had taken place. At the start of a six-month study on thirty women in 1990, he announced: "We think that if the pill is taken around twenty-four hours after ovulation, it can prevent pregnancy." Although it is too early to consider these tests scientifically definitive, the increasing possibility of RU 486 as a safe and effective contraceptive may provide an invaluable alternative to the high-frequency doses of the present birth control pills.

RU 486 FOR DIFFICULT BIRTHS

Already proved in European tests, RU 486 has become a critical factor in helping women through difficult deliveries. The drug may reduce numbers of cesareans as an alternative for those deliveries. At least one of every four U.S. births seems to require a cesarean section. Because of its anti-progesterone effect, RU 486 makes the uterus contract and thus speeds the opening of the cervix.

With RU 486 "opening the cervix very quickly, very thoroughly, and very reliably," Dr. Hodgen rates it "very useful in cases of difficult and prolonged labor." Dr. R. E. Garfield of McMaster University Hospital in Hamilton, Canada, praises "RU 486 treatment in combination with uterine stimulants" for increasing the "success rate of delivery in women."

In other aspects of delivery, RU 486 facilitates the extraction of ectopic embryos, abnormal fetuses, and fetuses that have died in the uterus. A research project at NIH used RU 486 "as a progesterone antagonist in order to induce and therefore study early labor and parturition." Further, RU 486 can be an essential supplement to late first-trimester abortions done by the suction method. By dilating the cervix, it can diminish the breaking of muscle fibers and cervical damage. Such damage can result from the need to dilate the cervix and introduce a cannula to ease the evacuation of residual products that cause bleeding and infection.

Throughout the third trimester of pregnancy, RU 486 and prostaglandin may become an alternative to surgery to end a pregnancy because of a badly malformed fetus or because the mother's health is threatened. This therapy in late pregnancy could be generally less risky than the kinds of surgery now performed. RU 486 and prostaglandin may also prove essential when the fetus dies in utero, greatly easing expulsion of the fetus.

Although such therapies have long benefited European women, the fanaticism that blocks RU 486 from U.S. hospitals, even for non-abortion uses, means that no American woman can be helped through a dangerous labor or delivered quickly of a dead or abnormal fetus.

RU 486 FOR CUSHING'S SYNDROME

Another example of a treatment denied the U.S. public is the use of RU 486 for Cushing's syndrome, a life-threatening condition that results from excessive production of the adrenal gland hormone, cortisol, and the abnormalities it causes in body tissue and blood chemistry. Although 80 percent of an estimated five hundred American victims annually can be helped by surgery, RU 486 has proved its value in hundreds of cases in recent years, and could eliminate the attendant risks of surgery in many more.

After preliminary testing on monkeys, Dr. George Chrousos at NIH found that RU 486 obstructed the injurious action of cortisol on target tissue. Starting in 1984 with humans, he showed that small, oral doses of one-half to one gram a day over a period of two to three months successfully inhibited the cortisol effect. Still, the NIH can handle only a limited number of cases because it gets an insufficient supply of RU 486. Not mentioning that many patients may be denied this treatment, the NIH report concludes: "Surgery is particularly hazardous for patients with Cushing's syndrome, and the use of RU 486 to correct the abnormalities caused by excessive cortisol before surgery should make the procedure safer and improve outcome."

RU 486 FOR BRAIN TUMORS

In another promising area of treatment, RU 486 has been used for meningioma, a primary tumor of the membrane that surrounds the brain and that often causes impaired mental function. "Brain tumors contain progesterone receptors," explains Dr. Daniel Philibert of Roussel. "The tumor's growth can be dependent on the receptor, and RU 486 as an anti-progesterone can probably slow it down."

Dr. Steven Grunberg, a University of Southern California oncologist, reports that RU 486 "happens to have the hormonal effect that we're looking for to treat this tumor." Grunberg and his team gave the compound to fourteen men and women with inoperable meningioma. In four patients, the tumor shrank about 10 percent. In six, it remained stable. Of three cases where the tumor progressed, two were referred out of the study for chemotherapy after their tumors proved malignant. One patient dropped out for personal reasons. Stressing that "in the skull even a few millimeters (of shrinkage) can make the difference between a major neurologic problem or not," Grunberg concludes, "We're very excited and encouraged because we feel that four have shown a response."

As a treatment for ENDOMETRIOSIS and ENDOMETRIAL CANCER, both involving the tissue lining of the

uterus, RU 486 proved in an NIH study to have a pro-
gesterone-blocking effect on the twenty-ninth day of the
menstrual cycle in cancers that may be enlarged by progesterone. Since the compound can be targeted at this
exact point, the study suggests that it might "inhibit the
growth" of both maladies. Uterine tissue grows aber-
rantly in endometriosis, the third leading cause of infertility among U.S. women, and research aims at improv-
ing the chances of female fertility.

"Since some OVARIAN CANCERS have progesterone
receptors," the NIH explains, "RU 486 might provide a
specific chemotherapy." Similarly, with BREAST CAN-
CER, the NIH believes that "in theory, fibrocystic disease
of the breast, which is stimulated by progesterone, should
also improve with RU 486 antagonism of progesterone
action." One study shows that the compound enhances
the strength of tamoxifen, an estrogen antagonist already
employed to slow down the growth of human breast
cancer cells.

The most disturbing aspect of all these potential uses
of RU 486 is how little testing is going on. Most of it has
been done by European scientists, and almost none has
been done in the United States except at NIH. And NIH
is limited by demands from extremists in Congress that
research must never touch the area of abortion.

The Roussel Company discouraged American research
by failing to make a suitable supply of the compound
available for tests. American scientists have been reluc-
tant to insist that their work deserves higher priority. Part
of the problem is Roussel's avoidance of U.S. political
turmoil surrounding RU 486 and its fear of religious boycotts. The company has also concentrated on maximizing

profits from European countries accepting RU 486 as an abortifacient.

Women have generally suffered. Except for its use in such all-inclusive areas as brain tumors or Cushing's syndrome, the broadest potential for research in RU 486 affects contraception, difficult births, and cancers that are solely female concerns.

As if the denial of a valuable abortifacient were not enough punishment, extremist groups in the United States have politicized every corollary function of RU 486 that could benefit women. Instead of demanding the independence of scientific research, the public has bowed to such pressures. National concentration on the AIDS disaster came about only through the militancy of the homosexual community, which may have been abrasive but brought results. It may be necessary for everyone dedicated to high standards of national health to raise the campaign for RU 486 research to the same pitch. The intrusion of political demagoguery into medicine now affects a range of procedures from fetal research to enforced cesareans. Stopping this trend has become a priority for all health organizations. Politics has no place in medicine. Politics must stop at a woman's skin.

Part Two
Why RU 486
Isn't Available in the
United States

7

The Maze of Abortion Politics

Considering the high level of national support for the right to abortion, the ability of extremists to keep RU 486 banned from the United States requires a searching examination of how the "pro-life" movement, consisting mainly of Catholics and Fundamentalists, achieves its political aims. Every poll confirms the pro-choice majority. Sixty-nine percent in the *New York Times*/CBS poll of September 1989 agreed with the statement: "Even in cases where you might think abortion is the wrong thing to do, the Government has no business preventing a woman from having an abortion."

The crucial question is how a small bloc of anti-abortion votes can exert such influence on the Reagan and Bush administrations and on enough members of Congress to block RU 486 not just from public use but even from government testing. The fear among politicians that an election can be lost by as few as five hundred to one thousand votes from a highly organized pressure group provides part of the answer. When that group represents an alliance of Catholics and Fundamentalists, and when it has made the destruction of abortion rights the target of an overall conservative campaign against such issues

as gun control and pornography, it can easily put together a bedrock number of legislators.

In addition, the extremism of Pope John Paul II has
pushed the American Catholic hierarchy to adopt an increasingly harder line. The pope cannot even yield on his
obsession with birth control. American Catholics (and
those Catholics in France, Italy, and other industrialized
countries) have long adopted birth control and cut their
family size to the same standards of other religions. Yet
the pope continues to demand a ban on contraception
when visiting Africa, where he is surrounded by the poverty and famine of such countries as Kenya, whose population has quadrupled since 1968. In Mexico on his 1990
tour, even with 40 percent of the Mexican people under
age fifteen and the government desperately trying to shrink
the population growth rate, the pope inveighed against
birth control.

Vatican appointments of conservative bishops in the
United States have intensified the Catholic campaign
against abortion. Rocked by a study showing that Catholics have a 30 percent higher rate of abortion than Protestants, the American hierarchy seems caught up in a
desperate campaign to make the destruction of abortion
rights a symbol that it can still dominate the actions of
its members. By 1990 the Catholic hierarchy's concentration on abortion had reached the stage where it ap-
peared to rank as the only issue on its agenda, this in the
face of increasing homelessness, growing poverty among
women and children, and the AIDS crisis.

The most significant evidence of the church's obsession is the hierarchy's plunge into election politics, in
which the church has risked breaking the law and losing

its tax-exempt status. Section 501(c)(3) of the U.S. Tax Code guarantees First Amendment separation of church and state by prohibiting any tax-exempt religious group from supporting or attacking political candidates. The separation principle has long been cherished by Catholic politicians. The only Catholic candidates for president, Governor Al Smith of New York in 1928 and John F. Kennedy in 1960, pledged themselves to it. Kennedy's pledge that "no Catholic prelate would tell the president, should he be a Catholic, how to act" undoubtedly became a critical factor in his slim margin of victory.

In a reversal of these historic precedents, the hierarchy in 1980 launched a string of challenges to the tax law. The official newspaper of the archdiocese of San Antonio, Texas, that year not only listed its favored candidates in an editorial, but taunted the IRS in its headline: "To the IRS NUTS!!!" Dozens of official Catholic papers since then, in places ranging from St. Cloud, Minnesota, and Jackson, Michigan, to Vienna, Virginia, have published lists of candidates to support or attack based on their stand on abortion.

The hierarchy obviously was counting on its influence with the Reagan-Bush administrations in its confrontation with the tax law. Twice before, in 1964, the IRS had punished Protestant groups—the *Christian Century*, a small journal, and Billy James Hargis's radio ministry, Christian Echoes—with the temporary loss of tax exemption for backing political candidates. But in 1980, when Abortion Rights Mobilization (ARM), a New York–based organization, brought Catholic violations to the attention of the IRS, that agency simply ignored them.

ARM went into federal court to make the IRS enforce

the law. Yet despite massive evidence, the case never went to trial. Instead, the IRS and the church deflected the central issue by protesting ARM's "standing," or right to sue. Although Protestant and Jewish clergy among ARM's plaintiffs insisted they qualified for standing due to the direct, serious injury that they suffered because Catholics had the advantage of using tax-exempt, political dollars, the Supreme Court turned them down.

Once the Catholic Church no longer risked losing its tax exemption, its political intervention in the abortion conflict became almost reckless. For example, in California just prior to the 1989 election, the bishop of San Diego announced that he would deny communion to a pro-choice assemblywoman running for state senate. The archbishop of Guam threatened to excommunicate any Catholic legislator who did not vote for a bill severely restricting abortion. In a climactic move reflecting the church's intent to whip every Catholic politician into line, Cardinal John O'Connor of New York City threatened to excommunicate any Catholic officeholder, including New York Governor Mario Cuomo, who refused to reverse a pro-choice position and publicly adhere to Catholic dogma.

The threat embodied the church's increasing confidence that Catholic legislators would soon be instrumental in defining national policy on abortion, including enforcement of the government's ban on RU 486. About 25 percent of Catholic House members and about 20 percent of the Senate, who already supported abortion rights or might eventually support them, would be affected.

The Catholic church, in effect, was tearing apart the two-hundred-year-old principle of church-state separation on which the country had been founded. It was saying that Catholic officeholders had to sacrifice their own convictions and often the consensus of a majority of their constituents in order to obey the bishops. It was saying that a Catholic candidate had to pledge himself or herself to church dogma before entering politics, which could eliminate many highly qualified Catholics from public service and destroy the tradition of American pluralism and harmonious relations among all religions.

Outraged at the church's threats, U.S. Senator Patrick J. Leahy (D-Vt.), a Catholic, concluded, "That's not acceptable in a country that's based on the First Amendment." Even U.S. Senator Dennis DeConcini (D-Ariz.), an opponent of abortion rights and also a Catholic, worried that "it does not help the promotion of Catholicism and its credibility. . . ."

The church's aggressiveness marked a total realignment of religious politics. For at least a century, the South and some Midwestern state like Indiana, where the Ku Klux Klan ruled, had been the seat of anti-Catholicism. But from 1980 on, as Catholic conservatives and Fundamentalists joined forces against abortion, many Catholic bishops decided that their best interests lay with a Republican White House and with Fundamentalists such as U.S. Senator Jesse Helms, a North Carolina Republican.

At one time, the church's influence stemmed from the immigrant vote and big-city political machines, but with affluent Irish- and Italian-Americans moving to the suburbs, the church lost much of its control in New York City, Chicago, and other cities, and had to find new allies.

New York State offers a prime example of church losses. Governor Cuomo, U.S. Senator Patrick Moynihan, and U.S. Representative Charles Rangel, a leading black politician, are all Catholics and all pro-choice. The Republican party, once the base of anti-abortion conservatives, picked a pro-choice candidate for governor in 1990 and approved a pro-choice party platform. Even U.S. Representative Susan Molinari of Staten Island, also a Catholic, has taken an abortion rights stand in opposition to her father who held the seat before her. Only U.S. Senator Alphonse D'Amato remains a holdout. Facing reelection in 1992, however, he has tempered his rigidity against abortion.

If there seem to be elements of irrationality in the Catholic concentration on abortion in the United States, they could stem from losses elsewhere. France, Italy, Spain, and lately Belgium have always been considered Catholic countries, but abortion rights there have become so accepted that the church has little chance of reversing their laws legalizing abortion. Catholic demonstrations and marches against RU 486 in France have dwindled away. The church, consequently, seems to have chosen the United States for its abortion battleground. The volcanic nature of American politics and the strength of the church's partnership with the White House and Fundamentalists have shaped a strategy that demands abortion be stopped in one dominant country.

The Catholic-Fundamentalist alliance has been encapsulated in the drive in the Louisiana state legislature in

1990 to pass the most stringent anti-abortion bill in the United States (after a similar bill in Idaho was vetoed by the governor). Despite an overwhelming coalition behind the bill of Fundamentalists from the northern and central parts of the state and Catholics from New Orleans and the south, the governor eventually vetoed the bill.

The Fundamentalists' opposition to abortion may be cloaked in biblical rhetoric (although the Bible never mentions birth control or abortion), but essentially springs from their attitude toward sex. They demand chastity before marriage as the foundation of family values. Although parents naturally have a right to promote chastity among their children, the statistical evidence on the nationwide sexual activity of teenagers makes this emphasis as unrealistic as the Fundamentalist vehemence against Darwinism and evolution. Both reflect the Fundamentalist anti-science stance.

"We must return to respect for chastity," preaches Judie Brown, president of the American Life Lobby. *Christianity Today*, an important Fundamentalist journal, calls for the "validity of virginity, the management of masturbation." State Senator Jim West (R-Spokane) has pushed this demand to absurdity by introducing a bill into the Washington state legislature, still pending, that would make it a crime for people under age eighteen to engage in sex, including "heavy petting." Offenders would be punished with ninety days in jail and a $5,000 fine, both of which could be lifted if they decide to marry.

The influence of Catholics and Fundamentalists on Congress was demonstrated in 1981 by the passage of the Adolescent Family Life Act, whose aim was to preserve the "integrity of the American family" and promote "self-discipline and other prudent approaches to the problems of adolescent, premarital sexual relations." Although the value of the bill's federal grants to churches and religious groups teaching chastity has never been verified, U.S. Senator Roger W. Jepsen (R-Iowa) hailed it as a bulwark against the "wave of humanism which has swept the country."

The Catholic-Fundamentalist emphasis on chastity hardly fits nationwide attitudes. A Gallup poll in 1987 found that forty-six percent of the public thought that premarital sex was wrong (27 percent thought so in the eighteen- to twenty-nine-year-old age group). Among Catholics, only 39 percent thought it was wrong.

The real agenda of the chastity bloc is not just an attack on abortion rights but a ban on birth control. Joseph Scheidler, head of the Pro-Life Action League, brands contraception as "disgusting, people using each other for pleasure," and proclaims: "We're opposed to all methods of birth control. We think the contraception mentality is a pro-abortion mentality."

"We are opposed to any government program or law that would allow distribution of birth control to the unmarried," declares the American Life League's Robert Marshall, who includes divorced and widowed people in that definition. Referring to RU 486, Douglas Johnson of the National Right to Life Committee insists that "any encouragement of contraceptive development might lead to a testing of such drugs." Despite statistics showing that abortions in France have declined since the introduction of RU 486, Johnson argues, "If you have a drug commonly available that makes abortion easier, you will have more abortions."

Such attacks on contraception further reveal the extent of Fundamentalist irrationality. Opponents of abortion should be promoting birth control to cut the number of abortions. Ninety percent of women use birth control successfully. But the three million who don't, and are annually at risk for unintended pregnancies (sexually active, fertile, not trying to get pregnant), make up one-half of the 1.6 million abortions each year.

Clinging to the concept of the "typical" American family of the last century, Fundamentalists fail to grasp that it is a disappearing species. Families consisting of a husband, a wife, and at least one child now comprise only 28 percent of all households. In the Fundamentalist ideological world, male power once reigned supreme. The loss of this power has stirred much of the anger now focused on abortion, but at a deeper level, that anger is aimed at the women's movement and the sexual revolution, which have tested and eroded male dominance.

The escape of women from age-old stereotypes and their quest for new educational and employment opportunities pose an alarming challenge that has put many men on the defensive. Their recourse is to keep women cloistered at home as the bedrock of family values. The most obvious restriction on women is to force them to bear a child against their will. The war on abortion and birth control thus protects and reinforces the sentence to bear children. By contrast, RU 486 guarantees women freedom of choice through a private, simple, and almost painless abortion—no punishment for women, no control for men.

The threat of new types of relationships not dependent on male power—single parenthood or relationships between unmarried people—intensifies the beleaguered status of Fundamentalism. Illustrating the fury it rouses were the signs carried by protesters against the Gay and Lesbian Pride March in New York in 1990. A group describing itself as born-again Christians demanded "Excommunication Now." Other signs warned: "Perverts on parade, someday you'll get AIDS."

Fundamentalists also vent their fury by blockading and invading abortion clinics. The Reverend Edward Markley, a Catholic priest, forced his way into a Birmingham, Alabama, clinic in 1985, smashing up surgery rooms and harassing a woman worker alone on the premises. He was tried and jailed, but his superior, Bishop Vath, seemed to support the act by declaring, "The right to life certainly supersedes the right to property and privacy." In 1990 in the New York area alone, federal courts, upheld by the U.S. Supreme Court, levied fines of $450,000 for illegal invasions of clinics, invasions that often had the tacit blessing of the hierarchy.

In trying to determine how the Catholic-Fundamentalist opposition translates into congressional votes, it is important to note that this bloc of about 14 percent is only one political force. At the other end is the bloc supporting abortion under all circumstances, which makes up about half the population in most polls. In between is the wavering center.

The center generally leans toward abortion rights, as shown by the September 1989 *New York Times*/CBS poll, with 69 percent against governmental interference in a woman's choice. The wavering center has reservations about specific areas—for example, it supports parental approval for a girl under age eighteen. Seventy percent of those responding to the same *Times* poll felt that such approval should be required. Thus, the Supreme Court's June 1990 decision in the *Hodgson v. Minnesota* case, in which it ruled 5 to 4 that approval for teenagers by both parents was constitutional because the state provides the alternative of a judicial hearing, would seem to follow public opinion.

Perhaps the most accurate measure of the electorate's influence is to examine how individual legislators have swung from anti-abortion to pro-choice positions. There have been switches the other way, but far fewer. In New York, Assemblyman John C. Dearie (D-Bronx) was banned from speaking at the Catholic church where he had worshiped for forty-six years, because he had voted for Medicaid abortion for the poor. More than two years later, in 1989, he switched his position after several private meetings with Cardinal O'Connor, whom he called his "spiritual guide." By contrast, State Senator Nicholas Spano (R-Yonkers), a Catholic who had unfailingly voted against abortion, came out for abortion rights in 1990, saying, "I was elected to be a member of the Senate, not to impose my personal philosophy on all people I represent." Spano comes from a district where pro-choice forces had just elected a congresswoman almost solely on the abortion issue.

The case of U.S. Representative Frank Pallone (D-NJ) demonstrates waning Catholic-Fundamentalist influence in a state that is 40 percent Catholic and where Fundamentalists, although few, have gained increasing control over the right-to-life movement. Pallone, a Catholic, had been anti-abortion for years as a New Jersey state senator. When the Republican congressman died in office,

Pallone won the seat in 1988 on an anti-abortion platform. Representing Monmouth County, a semi rural area,
he signed the anti-abortion brief in the critical *Webster v.
Reproductive Health Services* case before the Supreme Court,
urged the Democratic National Committee to change its
pro-choice stance, and was rated in the opposition on
every reproductive rights vote, according to the Population Crisis Committee's "rating chart."

But by 1989 abortion rights organizing was cutting into
the Catholic bloc. An Eagleton Institute-*Newark Star Ledger*
poll showed the state 80 percent pro-choice and only 8
percent completely opposed to abortion. Pallone reversed his position. When President Bush vetoed a bill
in 1990 that granted federal money for Medicaid abortion in cases involving rape or incest or to save a woman's life, Pallone joined the majority that overrode the
veto. Moreover, he won the Democratic primary handily
as a pro-choice candidate and became one of the early
sponsors of the Freedom of Choice Act, which would
guarantee abortion rights through congressional legislation.

New England presents the most significant evidence of
the erosion of the Catholic bloc. As early as November
1985, the voters of Bristol, Connecticut, a city with a 70
percent Catholic population, had the chance to decide in
a referendum whether or not they wanted to overturn
the Supreme Court decision legalizing abortion. Despite
the campaign by Catholic clergy in a working-class city,
abortion rights were supported by 56 percent.

The same pattern was repeated on election day in 1986.
In Rhode Island, a state with a 67 percent Catholic population, an anti-abortion referendum was defeated by 65

percent of the vote. In Massachusetts, which is about half Catholic and where the hierarchy waged an intense campaign, a similar referendum was defeated by 58 percent.

Climaxing this trend, the legislature of Connecticut, a state that is about 44 percent Catholic, passed a bill in 1990 that guarantees all abortion rights as defined in the Supreme Court's *Roe v. Wade* decision. Passed by the stunning margins of 136 to 12 in the House and 32 to 3 in the senate, the Connecticut law, according to many constitutional experts, could probably not be overthrown by the Supreme Court since its *Webster* decision has already given the states ample rein to legislate on abortion. In addition, courts in six states—California, Connecticut, Florida, Massachusetts, New Jersey, and Oregon—have already ruled that abortion rights are protected under the state constitutions.

All this evidence should jolt the White House. But a strange dichotomy grips the Republican leadership. Lee Atwater, chairman of the party's National Committee, certainly recognized the danger signs when he announced in January 1990 that Republican candidates would no longer be bound by the party's anti-abortion platform but could follow their consciences (and political instincts).

Why, then, has President Bush remained inflexible? He may, of course, overrate the power of Catholic bishops and Fundamentalist clergy, who have constant access to the executive office. He may still consider the hard-core vote of 14 percent so essential to his political base and that of his congressional followers that he cannot budge in his opposition to abortion, particularly on RU 486. The extremist bloc in Congress may be getting smaller, but members of Congress like Robert Dornan can rouse a storm against RU 486 far beyond their actual influence.

The critical 1990 elections should bring the president a new awakening. A referendum of Nevada voters, passed by 62 percent, stood behind the state's abortion rights law. A referendum in Oregon, attempting to ban abortions in almost all circumstances, was defeated by 68 per cent of the vote. In Oregon also, a restrictive requirement that minors must notify one parent before abortion was defeated by 52 per cent. In gubernatorial races in eight states, pro-choice governors replaced anti-abortion governors. Although U.S. Senate elections gave no clear-cut picture of a trend, abortion rights gained seven new supporters in the House of Representatives.

With pro-choice gains reaching an impressive level, Bush may take tentative steps similar to his shift on taxes. He could use indirect pressure to allow testing of RU 486 at four or five universities in addition to the University of Southern California where tests have halted. Despite the FDA's status as a scientific agency, the White House still influences its politically sensitive decisions. The president could use this influence to allow the FDA to explore the compound for its contraceptive possibilities, and put real money behind research into its side uses for cancer. But the chances of a policy being developed that would allow a drug company to import, test, and market RU 486 with FDA approval are slim. Bush, as well as the extremists, knows that distribution of RU 486 throughout the United States could mean the end of anti-abortion fervor. Only a Democratic president offers a real possibility of change.

8

"Social Civil War" over RU 486

The conflict over RU 486 has produced a pall of fear at the National Institutes of Health (NIH), the U.S. government's huge center in Maryland. Slapping a pile of notebooks, holding angry letters from conservative members of Congress demanding that no federal funds be spent on anything resembling abortifacient research, George Gaines, an NIH executive, admits, "Our scientists are under great pressure."

As victims of what the *Tampa Tribune & Times* calls a "social Civil War," NIH research projects are hamstrung by White House restrictions on abortion and constant threats from extremist senators and representatives. Scientists are forbidden by NIH executives to use their names in interviews on RU 486 involving abortion. A test examining nothing more dangerous than the effect of RU 486 on pregnancy achieved a note of absurdity when scientists were banned from performing abortion on the test monkeys.

"The easy way to do this study to determine if there was a safe dose of RU 486 to use in pregnancy for its anti-glucocorticoid affects," laments the official report, "would have been to use pregnant monkeys. Instead, in order to avoid possible abortion in monkeys, hormones were administered to castrated monkeys to simulate pregnancy. This made it possible, though more difficult, to do this important study."

The stifling of abortion research by the Reagan and Bush administrations has also impeded research on imperative medical therapy. New research that could benefit up to half a million American sufferers of Parkinson's, a progressive and debilitating disease, has been stopped because of research links to abortion. After Swedish scientists at the University of Lund demonstrated that dopamine-producing brain cells from aborted fetuses created marked improvement in Parkinson's victims when injected into their brains, a "blue ribbon" commission hailed it as a significant advance. "Every indication is that maladies such as Parkinson's disease, Huntington's disease, childhood diabetes, and perhaps Alzheimer's disease can be considerably improved by the use of such tissue," reported Judge Arlen M. Adams, the commission chair.

Still, the White House banned fetal cell implants, and the U.S. Department of Health and Human Services had to abandon its testing. "It's like the Middle Ages," observed Dr. Birt Harvey, president of the American Academy of Pediatrics, who attacked the White House for stopping "new knowledge that is going to save the lives of fetuses, babies, and adults as well."

The White House has consistently curtailed family planning and population policies that have any link to abortion. Starting in 1984 under Reagan and continuing under Bush, even private health agencies overseas could get no funding from the U.S. Agency for International Development unless they certified they would not perform or promote abortion. Bush vetoed a Foreign Operations Appropriations Bill in 1989 because it contained a small grant to the United Nations Fund for Population Activities, whose abortion guidelines did not conform with those of the White House.

Reversing previous positions on population control by Congress, James Buckley, Reagan's chief delegate at the UN's International Conference on Population at Mexico City in 1984, insisted that runaway population growth "in itself presents no problems." With free market economics, Buckley pronounced, soaring birthrates would become immaterial even in the poorest countries. A. W. Clausen, president of the World Bank, told the conference in rebuttal that the "evidence is overwhelming that rapid population growth impedes efforts to raise living standards in most of the developing world." In a Gallup poll a month before, 90 percent of Americans supported this assessment. Still, the Reagan administration clung to what was labeled "voodoo demographics," supported at the conference only by the North Yemen delegation.

The restrictive White House policy on family planning draws its political leverage from extremist boycotts aimed not only at abortion, but at birth control as well. In 1981, the Catholic-Fundamentalist alliance launched a campaign against the Planned Parenthood clinic in Allentown, Pennsylvania, to block its funding by United Way philanthropies, claiming Planned Parenthood was "showering these young people with contraceptive and provocative literature" and with "amoral and anti-Christian sex education programs." Subsequently, the alliance drove twelve Planned Parenthood clinics out of the United Way.

Boycotts have been particularly successful in radio and television, where executives dread negative mail from even the smallest pressure group. In 1987, the Association of Reproductive Health Professionals submitted a thirty-second paid television spot whose relatively innocuous theme was "change"—a few scenes of a crescent moon becoming a full moon and similar phenomena, ending with the phrase, "The birth control pill has gone through a lot of changes in twenty-five years." Although a Louis Harris poll showed that only 11 percent of Americans have any religious or moral objections to family planning, all three TV networks buckled under a handful of complaints and turned down the spot.

The main focus of the boycotts has been the drug companies. What worries them most is possible loss of sales. They are desperately afraid of controversy, of anything that could tarnish their image as highly professional dispensers of health. Both factors were involved when the National Right to Life Committee a few years ago boycotted the prostaglandins produced by the Upjohn Company of Michigan. Upjohn had already pulled out of research in contraceptives, and now removed its prostaglandins from the market and restricted their use to a handful of hospitals. Since prostaglandin has proved valuable in easing difficult childbirths and in other therapies in addition to its use with RU 486, Upjohn was denying the medical profession a drug critical to non-abortion emergencies.

The National Right to Life Committee hailed the success of its boycott. But Robert McDonough, an Upjohn executive, demurred: "Boycotts of Upjohn sponsored by anti-abortion activists were not a factor in our decision.

These boycotts have had no measurable effect on Upjohn sales."

In the case of its threatened boycott of Cytotec, the National Right to Life Committee was even more callous in its potential damage to medicine. Produced by G.D. Searle & Co. of Illinois and recently approved for marketing by the Food and Drug Administration, Cytotec has made a marked contribution to the treatment of bleeding ulcers, the primary cause of death among seven thousand patients in the United States annually, a secondary cause in ten thousand more. Cytotec has long been a therapy in forty-three other countries.

Although Cytotec, a weak abortifacient, has never been tested for abortion, the National Right to Life Committee branded it a "death drug." Claiming that the drug was inessential in ulcer treatment, Dr. John Willke, the committee's president, suggested coated aspirin would protect the stomach just as well. Searle, which produces oral contraceptives, perhaps the committee's real target, has so far resisted threats. "The right to life does not begin or end at conception," points out Bill Greener, a senior vice president of the company. "People with ulcers have a right to life, too."

Continuing a campaign that U.S. Representative Patricia Schroeder (D-Colo.) has defined as "medical McCarthyism," the National Right to Life Committee has even demanded that its supporters cut off their memberships in and contributions to the National Audubon Society, Friends of the Earth, and other wildlife and environmental groups. The startling basis of this boycott is that these groups have become too concerned about soaring world population and its impact on natural re-

sources, and, consequently, opposed Reagan-Bush restrictions on U.S. aid to family planning overseas.

The ultimate campaign of nonsense was launched by
the Reverend Kenneth Dupin of the Valley View Wes-
leyan Church in Roanoke, Virginia, who urged congre-
gations in his area to boycott all French products since
RU 486 came from France. "Even things like escargot,"
the minister preached. "French people are still some of
the primary producers of snails for restaurants. And French
wines, of course."

Whether these boycotts have damaged the drug companies or not, the very threat of controversy, particularly
White House opposition, often paralyzes their actions. This
is certainly the case for Roussel, which by 1990 had shown
no interest in entering the U.S. market with RU 486.
Hoechst, its parent company, amasses one-fourth of its
annual $23 billion in sales in America and refuses to en-
danger these hefty profits. Roussel has obviously decided
there are enough profits from RU 486 in Europe for the
moment. It rates Italy and Spain far more stable markets
than the United States, where conflagration would be
stirred well before the first RU 486 pill was dispensed.

A secondary impact of the Catholic-Fundamentalist
boycott has been the decimation of contraceptive research. Once the Reagan and Bush administrations
downgraded the importance of birth control, the budget
for developments of new birth control techniques at the
U.S. National Institutes of Health remained static at $8
million for almost a decade, a puny sum considering that
the development of a new contraceptive takes ten to seventeen years and costs $30 million to $70 million.

This impact has also affected drug companies. In 1970, twenty major companies in the United States were involved in contraceptive development. Now there is only one. None of the active progestational and estrogenic ingredients of the birth control pill is manufactured today in the United States. Professor Carl Djerassi of Stanford University, who synthesized the ingredients of the first pill, labels the United States the "only country other than Iran in which the birth control clock has been set backward in the past decade."

A report from the National Academy of Sciences in 1990, developed by an expert panel headed by Dr. Luigi Mastroianni, chair of the Department of Obstetrics and Gynecology at the University of Pennsylvania Hospital, concludes that the "outlook for a new contraceptive development is bleak." It asserts that "many European countries are years ahead of the U.S. in the development of further contraceptive advances such as reversible male and female sterilization, a once-a-month pill that induces menstruation, and methods that interfere with sperm production."

A glaring example of contraceptive neglect is the long-delayed introduction of Norplant into the United States. Norplant consists of six tiny capsules of the progestin levonorgestrel (a sex hormone), which are implanted painlessly and quickly with local anesthesia under a woman's skin. Acting to inhibit ovulation and thicken cervical mucus, it protects a woman against pregnancy with a minuscule failure rate for the remarkable length of five years. Another advantage is reversibility—the capsules can be removed painlessly in a few minutes and the woman becomes fertile almost immediately. Since Norplant has no estrogen, some of the potential risks of the standard birth control pill are eliminated.

Norplant has been tested in forty-four countries for at least a dozen years and has been officially approved and used by 500,000 women in sixteen countries, including Bangladesh, China, Czechoslovakia, and Sweden. Yet the irony is that although it was developed in New York by the Population Council, Norplant has been tested only recently in the United States and did not gain official approval from the FDA until 1990.

The drug companies themselves prefer to attribute their retreat from contraceptive development more to the rising cost of lawsuits than to boycott threats and government obstacles (the cumbersome testing requirements of the FDA, among them). The most notorious lawsuit was an action brought against the Dalkon Shield, an IUD produced by the A. H. Robins Company. Significantly, Dalkon was marketed before such devices had to go through the FDA's approval process. Charging that Dalkon had produced pelvic inflammation, infection, infertility, miscarriage, and even death, more than 100,000 women filed claims in court and in 1990 won $2.5 billion in a Dalkon Trust Fund to be divided among claimants. Robins had to go into bankruptcy, and was taken over by another drug company.

The G. D. Searle Company lost a $8.75 million judgment to a woman claiming injury from its Copper-7, another IUD. Another woman won $5,151,000 from the Ortho Pharmaceutical Company after using its spermicide, Ortho-Gynol, not knowing that she was pregnant. She claimed that it caused birth defects in her child. All told, twelve major lawsuits have been won against drug manufacturers in recent years. Yet these companies' losses (excluding Robins') amount to only about 1 percent of their total sales from contraceptives, raising the suspicion that the companies are more concerned about preserving their image of inviolability than about the short-term damage to their pocketbooks.

To counteract the timidity of the drug manufacturers, particularly the Roussel Company's fear of a boycott aimed at its American sales, the family planning and women's movements began organizing in 1989 to build public momentum behind RU 486. That year a banner headline in the National Organization for Women's *Times* announced: "Feminists Vow to Bring Abortion Pill to America." NOW's "Freedom Caravan" confronted officials of Hoechst (Roussel's majority stockholder) at its Bridgewater, New Jersey, plant, and the caravan moved on to Pennsylvania, Massachusetts, Nevada, Oregon, and other states, gathering well over 100,000 petition signatures to present to Roussel. Organizations from the National Black Women's Health Project to the American Jewish Congress passed resolutions supporting the pill. A Louis Harris poll showed that 59 percent of the country favored distribution of RU 486 in the United States.

The RU 486 campaign was coordinated by Reproductive Health Technologies of Washington, a consortium of organizations that includes the Planned Parenthood Federation and the American College of Obstetricians and Gynecologists. Planned Parenthood's objective has been to organize medical experts and gain influence with the media. At a series of meetings in 1990 held at the Baylor College of Medicine in Texas, the University of Southern

California in Los Angeles, and the Boston Museum of Science (cosponsored by Harvard's Medical School and School of Public Health), Planned Parenthood brought together prominent scientists and politicians to promote new birth control methods and RU 486. Addressed by such speakers as U.S. Representatives Barbara Boxer (D-Cal.) and Patricia Schroeder (D-Colo.), these meetings aimed to enlist medical schools to pressure the government for expanded testing of RU 486.

The editorial pages of the daily press in the last few years were almost unanimously behind RU 486. Calling the advantages of the pill "so clear-cut that it cannot long be denied American women," the *Boston Globe* insisted, "It is unrealistic to envision women through the world having access to RU 486, while American women are denied it." The *Washington Post* urged that "neither this government nor the French manufacturer should let political considerations delay that [approval] process." After pointing out that "clearly, then, there is an American market for RU 486," the *New York Times* asked, "Now where's the marketer?"

Abortion would become a torrid issue at the annual meeting of the American Bar Association in Chicago in August 1990. After the ABA's House of Delegates a few months before had voted 238 to 106 for a resolution supporting a woman's constitutional right to abortion, ad hoc groups opposed to the resolution began organizing from the Chicago headquarters of Americans United for Life Legal Defense Fund, an anti-abortion base. Both sides campaigned for votes in the 385,000-member association.

Outspending pro-choice lawyers 10 to 1 in their lobbying, opponents of the resolution convinced the House of Delegates that August to reject its previous stand by a 200 to 188 vote. Although the ABA had taken positions before on such controversial issues as the Equal Rights Amendment, the House agreed that abortion was so "extremely divisive" that no position should be taken.

Nothing, however, is more crucial to the introduction of RU 486 than the weight of the medical profession. Leading the way in a March 1990 resolution, the California Medical Association voted overwhelmingly for the pill's admission to the country. "It is in keeping with basic medical standards to avoid surgical procedures whenever an equally effective non-invasive alternative is available," the association pointed out. At its June meeting, the American Medical Association's House of Delegates, representing 290,000 doctors nationwide, took an almost identical position in a voice vote that Dr. Charles Sherman, its chair, called "unanimous in [its] approval on this issue."

Despite all these pressures, the White House had given no hint of yielding on RU 486 by the fall of 1990. The Food and Drug Administration simply reflects administration policy. Referring to RU 486 in its directive of June 6, 1989, the agency ruled that "unapproved products of this kind would be inappropriate for release under the personal importation policy. The intended use of such drugs could pose a risk to the safety of the user."

The FDA's decision, of course, was absurd on a scientific level. The pill had not only been proved safe in 50,000 French cases and in thousands more in Britain and other countries, but FDA scientists, who had seen the French data, considered it eminently qualified for approval.

Troubled that the FDA was becoming a political rather than a scientific agency, a number of House committees considered an investigation. U.S. Representative Ron Wyden (D-Ore.) held hearings in November 1990. U.S. Representative Ted Weiss (D-N.Y.), who headed a Subcommittee of Government Operations, requested pertinent documents from FDA files for hearings in late 1990. Referring to the president's nomination of a director of the National Institutes of Health, U.S. Representative Henry Waxman (D-Cal.), chair of the House Subcommittee on Health and the Environment, charged that "in attempts to cater to the extremists of the anti-abortion lobby, the White House has used the candidates' positions on abortion and fetal research as a litmus test for any appointments."

In terms of the damage of the extremist attack on abortion, no group has proved more vulnerable than the medical profession. No group would gain more security from RU 486's admission to the United States. Doctors have been the targets of the same violence as their patients. Their clinics have been invaded, bombed, and burned. Their personal lives, and those of their spouses and children, have often turned into a nightmare. The toll has been so great that many physicians are forced to give up their abortion practice and move to another city or town, leaving an increasing number of areas of the country with no abortion service whatsoever.

The introduction of RU 486 into the United States could help to solve this problem. If doctors could give the pill in the privacy of their office, without the glare of publicity, abortion would become as routine as the administration of an antibiotic. Doctors would be spared the picketing and invasion of their clinics and the resultant political turmoil.

The effect of the present violence against the medical profession can be measured in statistics from the American College of Obstetrics and Gynecology. Although 85 percent of its members in a 1985 study supported the legality of abortion, only a third actually performed it, and only 2 percent did more than twenty-five abortions a month (mainly clinic doctors, assumedly). Many doctors, avoiding abortion despite supporting it, may have had personal objections, but the majority may have refused to become entangled in harassment. The *New York Times* in an January 1990 editorial stressed that with RU 486, "abortion would be as private a decision as it should be, and the procedure being non-surgical, considerably safer."

The attacks on Dr. Eduardo Aquino and his clinic in Corpus Christi, Texas, "disrupted my life and terrorized my wife and four children," he related. Although his unlisted home phone number was constantly changed, threats poured in to his wife, Mercedes. On March 1, 1988, a dozen screaming picketers surrounded their house. When Dr. Aquino arrived, his wife "was crying and hysterical, barely able to tell me what was going on." Their ten-year-old son, Eddie, had locked himself in his room.

The house was surrounded twice more in March, and a bomb threat was telephoned to Aquino's clinic. "Fear was tearing my family apart," he said. "Mercedes sank into depression, crying in our bedroom for hours during the day." The grades of their eldest son, Eddie, plummeted, and he became uncontrollable. "Eddie had to be hospitalized for his behavioral disorders. In June, on his psychiatrist's recommendation, we arranged to have Eddie stay indefinitely with my sister-in-law in Paraguay. Under the stress, Mercedes' peptic ulcer flared up, and she had to be treated for that as well as post-traumatic stress syndrome."

Although the doctor has won monetary damages in court against this terrorism, which are being appealed, the family's suffering persists. His wife is "afraid of elevators, planes, people—almost everything," he said. When the doctor is called out at night, "she turns off the air conditioner while she waits so she can hear every sound. She sees a psychiatrist every week, but I fear she'll never regain her spirit." Eddie has been held back in school and also sees a psychiatrist. Dr. Aquino, despite excommunication by the bishop of Corpus Christi, continues to do abortions at his clinic and office.

Dr. Curtis Boyd of Albuquerque, New Mexico, has been the target of similar terrorism. Death threats are "routine" for him and his wife. They receive regular bomb threats. At his previous clinic in Dallas, Texas, "members of Operation Rescue charged the door, knocking a counselor and doctor to the ground before chaining themselves to the furniture and medical equipment," he recalls. On Christmas Eve 1988, the Dallas clinic was doused with gasoline and set ablaze, causing $100,000 worth of damage. But only one staff member quit. "For the rest of us," he says, "the arson was a reminder (a frightening and painful one, to be sure) how important it is that we have the courage to go on."

Dr. Boyd, who comes from pioneer Texas stock and was a captain in the Corps of Cadets at Texas A&M University, remembers that "my grandfather was an elder in the Foot Washing Baptist Church. I went to church with him every service. I grew up in a time when women and children were the property of men. That time is past." He speaks of a patient for whom he did an abortion many years ago. Now forty-two years old with two boys, ages four and nine, she wrote in a recent Christmas card that "you make it possible for so many women to have healthy families." "That is why I do abortions," he concludes. "I believe that the availability of abortions allows more women to create healthy families."

Dr. Peter Bours, bearded and sandy-haired, with intense blue eyes, has run an abortion practice for a decade in Forest Grove, Oregon, a small college and farming town of 11,500 population. Coming from a family long committed to family planning, he graduated from Stanford University in 1965, became a Phi Beta Kappa his junior year, and got his medical degree from Harvard. After years of death threats, one letter promised the doctor would be decapitated and his head left in a public place for people to urinate on. He had to move his wife and two children fifty miles away. On Mother's Day weekend in 1984, two firebombs were ignited against the walls of his clinic. Instead of dissuading him, the attack made him give up the family practice he had always conducted and concentrate on birth control, voluntary sterilization, and abortion.

Dr. Amy Cousins represents a new model: a doctor who volunteers to do abortions when a clinic cannot replace a retired medical director. Since no local doctor in Binghamton, New York, would fill the opening, Cousins drives two hundred miles from her home in New York City every Thursday, and after two days of duty at

Southern Tier Women's Services, drives back Friday evening. On Wednesday or Saturday, she again drives two hours to fill the medical shortage at a clinic in Allentown, Pennsylvania.

A graduate of Brown University, where she was first in her class, and of Harvard Medical School, the thirty-eight-year-old red-haired doctor gave up a flourishing Park Avenue practice in obstetrics and gynecology after having delivered two thousand babies. Since Binghamton was near the hometown of Randall Terry, founder of Operation Rescue, Cousins' clinic has been a prime target. There have been death threats, bomb threats, and constant invasions of the premises. Once a pregnant nurse was punched in the stomach. The pressure became so intense that Cousins put up her own money to have a six-foot-tall chain-link fence built around the clinic.

Cousins' commitment to abortion rights came slowly. Her only early exposure, at age eight, was when a relative had to search out an underground doctor in New Jersey accompanied by Cousins's mother and grandfather. "We didn't know if this woman would come back," she remembers. Once abortion was legalized in New York in 1970 and nationwide in 1973, Cousins belonged to a generation that took the right of choice for granted. "We thought that right could never be taken away—it would be like taking away the woman's vote," she says.

Her mother, widowed early, had to find a job to support three daughters and instilled in them a sense of feminine independence. One of Cousins's sisters is a psychiatrist, the other a lawyer. When Cousins started her obstetrical practice in New York, she had to support her office at first by doing occasional abortions at a nearby clinic. "I was just being medical and professional. I didn't see it as a cause yet," she points out.

Then the Binghamton clinic staff begged her to join them, and she accepted. As she talks about intruders forcing their way into her clinic, her voice becomes angry. "I just decided I wasn't going to cower in my office," she concludes. "It makes me furious when some patients—upstate New York and Allentown are conservative areas—tell me abortion is wrong, but it's okay when they need it. It makes me furious when doctors shirk their medical responsibility and plead with me to handle their abortion cases. It's none of a doctor's business what a woman decides to do with any pregnancy. He is there to see that she is safe and healthy."

Recently Cousins has moved aggressively against clinic attacks. Working with groups at the local State University of New York, she has developed an emergency system in which students rush to the defense of the clinic if an invasion starts, escorting patients through the picket lines. With her sister as legal counsel, she has secured a restraining order in federal court giving the police added authority to keep picketers a reasonable distance from the clinic entrance—an order enhanced by the U.S. Supreme Court decision *Terry v. New York NOW* of May 21, 1990, involving other New York clinics. Cousins sums up her credo: "I decided I just couldn't let fanatics impose their will on me."

Such terrorism may be a large factor in dissuading doctors from serving at abortion clinics, but there is a special problem in smaller cities and rural areas. In a hometown setting, where everyone scrutinizes a doctor's life, neighbors may shun a practitioner who has any links to abortion. The result is that most parts of the country offer no abortion services whatsoever, and women must travel hundreds of miles—a particular burden and expense for the poor—to find an abortion clinic.

In fact, only 27,400 abortions were done in non-metropolitan areas in 1988 compared with 1,563,400 in metropolitan areas, according to the Alan Guttmacher Institute. Eighty-three percent of the counties in the country—up from 78 percent in 1982—had no abortion services. That means that 31 percent of all women aged 15 to 44 had no local access to abortion. Ninety-two percent of counties, where 42 percent of women live, have no large-scale abortion facility.

Only one county of all counties in South Dakota has an abortion provider; only two counties in Kentucky, Nebraska, Delaware, Mississippi, North Dakota, and West Virginia have providers.

If RU 486, therefore, were introduced into the United States, it could make two critical contributions: it could provide abortion services in those counties that have none at present, and it could give doctors in those unserviced counties the protection and anonymity they would undoubtedly require in order to become abortion providers in their own offices.

The administration of RU 486 in the United States may well differ from the French system of government-approved hospitals and clinics, ostensibly structured to deal with the possibility of hemorrhage. But since the number of hemorrhage cases in France has been minuscule, this decision was undoubtedly made to give Roussel closer control over the compound and keep RU 486 abortions (like vacuum abortions) integrated into the French social security system.

Doctors who administer RU 486 in the United States in their offices should have a backup hospital nearby, and should check the identity and level of responsibility of the patient to ensure that she returns a day or two later for the prostaglandin dose and remains under observation. Surely the medical profession, which prescribes drugs far more sensitive than RU 486, can deal with a minimal possibility of risk. In the present turmoil roused by Catholic and Fundamentalist efforts to crush all abortion rights, RU 486 offers the best possibility to preserve and extend these rights. The privacy of the physician and the patient becomes paramount.

9

Privacy: "Most Comprehensive of Rights"

T he late Justice Louis Brandeis in 1928 may have called privacy the "most comprehensive of rights and the most valued by civilized man," but it remains an elusive issue in the United States. The country seems to support it overwhelmingly. A study by Louis Harris & Associates in 1981 found that 76 percent of Americans considered the right of privacy as important as "life, liberty, and the pursuit of happiness." The Supreme Court has guaranteed privacy in one aspect or another for almost one hundred years, but has never come to grips with an encompassing definition.

Yet the privacy of women's bodies has become a growing target for governmental intrusion. In one of numerous cases, a Chicago court in 1984 ordered a woman to have a cesarean delivery, although she and her husband refused. The husband was forcibly removed from the hospital by security officers. The woman was cuffed to four corners of the bed before delivery. A 1987 medical study listed thirty-six hospital attempts in eighteen states in the previous five years to force such medical decisions on women.

In 1987, when a pregnant women dying of cancer in a Washington, D.C., hospital refused to have a cesarean and was supported by her husband, family, and personal doctor, the hospital went to court and the court ordered it anyway. The baby died soon after, the mother a few days later.

The concept behind such invasions of privacy, as formulated by John Robertson, a University of Texas Law School professor, is that once a fetus has become viable, the state can appropriate a woman's body and subject her to criminal and civil liability for any accidental harm she might have done the fetus or judgmental error she might have made before the infant's birth. This dubious concept was carried to extraordinary lengths in the case of a California woman in 1986. Arrested for failing to follow medical advice during pregnancy, which the state insisted brought about the death of her brain-damaged infant, she spent six days in jail before charges were dropped.

This trend toward control by the state of a woman's reproductive life accentuates the need for the privacy in abortion guaranteed by RU 486. The guarantee of privacy is an essential part of the campaign by the women's movement to introduce the pill into the United States. It will be ironic, indeed, if the American movement, which has surpassed the movements in France, Britain, and many European countries in size and militancy, is continually denied the pill while many European women have access to it.

Because privacy is not mentioned specifically in the Constitution, conservative scholars have argued against the constitutionality of privacy which was basic to the *Roe v. Wade* decision legalizing abortion in 1973. Robert Bork, for example, took this position during Senate hearings on his qualifications for the Supreme Court. The possibility that *Roe* could be overthrown or seriously curtailed even imperils the *Griswold v. Connecticut* decision of 1965, which wiped out any potential for state intervention against birth control.

These conservative definitions of constitutionality fail to take into account that the right to privacy was first protected under the common law, which the American colonies inherited from England and which is still the underpinning of our judicial system. In fact, English common law for almost five hundred years protected the right of abortion before "quickening." Sir William Blackstone (1723–1780), whose *Commentaries* were a dominant influence on early U.S. law, described "quickening" as follows: "Life begins in contemplation of law as soon as the infant is able to stir in the mother's womb."

Since only the mother and possibly her husband could testify in court as to the moment of quickening, it was a vague demarcation point. Still, it remained U.S. law until shortly before the Civil War, when some states, under pressure from the medical profession, began to legislate against abortion to protect women from the health hazards of disreputable abortionists and inadequate medical techniques.

Privacy is a visionary concept that touches almost every aspect of the human condition and springs from the deepest personal needs. In a noted *Harvard Law Review* article in 1890, Brandeis, future Supreme Court justice, and the Boston lawyer Samuel Warren explored the philosophic ramifications of privacy. They defined it primarily as the right of "being left alone." They built their argument around the individual's "inviolate personality," summing up in these two words the doctrine that neither the government nor anyone else could intrude on the freedom and realm of living space that allow people to achieve their full potential as long as the rights of others are not damaged.

The Supreme Court dealt with many aspects of privacy from 1886 on before it grappled with reproductive privacy—yet, significantly, it drew on the *Boyd* case eighty years later in affirming the right of contraception. *Boyd v. United States* in 1886 ruled that a government subpoena for business records violated the "sanctity of a man's home and the privacies of life." The Court seemed to be affirming the Brandeis-Warren concept, as well as upholding common law, in *Union Pacific Railway Company v. Botsford* in 1891, when it deemed "sacred" the individual's common law right "to the possession and control of his own person, free from all restraint or interference by others, unless by clear and unquestionable authority of law."

This decision could be considered a broad protection of privacy. Yet it left undefined the exact limitations of the government's power to intrude—an evasion, which might almost be called a fear, of meeting the privacy issue head-on. Characteristically, in future decisions the Court preferred to approach privacy step by step, situation by situation.

Thus, the Court eventually dealt with broad aspects of sexual privacy—protecting the privacy of an individual to view pornography at home without governmental intrusion, for example. In *Stanley v. Georgia*, Justice Thurgood Marshall ruled for the majority: "Our whole constitutional heritage rebels at the thought of giving government the power to control men's minds." Yet the Court has been less conclusive in protecting the privacy of sexual preference. Neither in *Bowers v. Hardwick* in 1986 nor in prior decisions has it given adult, consenting homosexuals the power to control their bodies or sexual inclinations and practices even in their own homes.

When the Court finally came to grips in 1965 with privacy of choice in childbearing, its language was so encompassing that it was hard to believe that privacy rights could ever be eroded again. *Griswold v. Connecticut,* which overthrew the state's restrictive birth control law, draws broadly on what Justice William Douglas called in the majority opinion a "zone of privacy created by several fundamental constitutional guarantees." Citing the Fourth and Fifth Amendments "as protection against all governmental invasions 'of the sanctity of a man's home and the privacies of life' " (drawing a quotation from *Boyd* in 1886), he singled out the Fourth Amendment as creating a "right of privacy, no less important than any other right carefully reserved to the people." Justice Arthur J. Goldberg in another majority opinion in *Griswold* described the "right of privacy as fundamental and basic—a personal right 'retained by the people' within the meaning of the Ninth Amendment."

The Court further pinned down choice in childbearing in *Eisenstadt v. Baird* in 1972. "If the right of privacy means anything," Justice William Brennan declared for the majority, "it is the right of the individual, married or single, to be free from unwarranted governmental intrusion into matters so fundamentally affecting a person as the decision whether to bear or beget a child."

In its epic decision in 1973, *Roe v. Wade,* the Court

extended the right of privacy to abortion. Justice Harry Blackmun concluded in the majority opinion: "The right of privacy, whether it be founded in the Fourteenth Amendment's concept of personal liberty and restrictions upon state action, as we feel it is, or, as the District Court determined in the Ninth Amendment's reservation of rights to the people, is broad enough to encompass a woman's decision whether or not to terminate her pregnancy."

With a noteworthy, century-long record of privacy decisions behind it, the Court's 5 to 4 decision in *Webster v. Reproductive Health Services* in 1989 brought a disturbing dilution of past precedents. Not that the Court has failed to reverse or modify its decisions previously or been influenced by political forces. Before the Civil War Abraham Lincoln accused the Court of "conspiracy" to protect and extend slavery. Still, the principle of *stare decisis*—building on past precedents—has always been the bedrock of our legal system. Without it, rational decision-making becomes difficult, and society lacks standards to guide it.

By expanding the states' ability to set tighter restrictions on abortion, *Webster* reversed decades of privacy rights established in *Griswold, Roe,* and other cases. Justice Blackmun in his minority opinion, in fact, complained he could not recall a Court decision that "so foments disregard for the law and for our standing decisions."

Webster is based on "originalism"—William Rehnquist's insistence (and Robert Bork's, of course) that the Court must adjudicate only from the text of the Constitution and the intention of the framers, and that any right not explicitly stated in the Constitution cannot be protected.

If originalism becomes the ruling doctrine, the Court will never be able to grapple with the scientific and technological discoveries that are exerting increasing pressure on previous limitations on privacy. As medical progress, to cite one example, now keeps the critically ill alive often well beyond their own wish for survival, a growing consensus insists that privacy must include control of one's death as well as one's life. The host of religious and philosophic complexities involved in the right to die will soon challenge the courts even more intensely than the present debate over abortion.

Following a number of state court rulings on comatose patients, notably *In Re Quinlan* in New Jersey, the Supreme Court in 1990 ruled that a comatose patient can be removed from life-sustaining treatment only after "clear and convincing" evidence that before an accident or illness the patient had wanted such treatment stopped. But it was a state court that affirmed decisively the rights of a cognitive patient. Larry McAfee, a thirty-three-year-old quadriplegic who had been maimed and paralyzed as a result of a motorcycle accident, was being kept alive in a Georgia hospital through a respirator. His mind was completely lucid. Hiring a lawyer to argue that the machine "is not prolonging his life, but is instead prolonging his death," McAfee asked the court for the right to detach his respirator. A superior court judge ruled in his favor, and the case was taken directly to the Georgia Supreme Court. On November 21, 1989, a unanimous court supported McAfee's right to control his own death, but set no guidelines for the method or device that would place responsibility on McAfee for detaching the respirator.

It was a portentous case, the most sweeping affirmation by a state supreme court of the rights of a cognitive patient. But it was even more important because the judges based their decision not only on federal privacy precedents, but on the privacy laws of Georgia as well.

An equally impressive step had been taken six weeks before in Florida. On October 4, 1989, the state supreme court overthrew by 6 to 1 a restrictive law requiring parental consent for teenage abortion. This time the decision was based solely on the Florida Constitution, which guarantees an individual the "right to be let alone and free from governmental intrusion into his [or her] private life."

Both the Georgia and Florida cases portend a new momentum in state courts involving the protection of abortion rights and privacy rights in general under state constitutions. There is a decided advantage in this trend. Unless it is in direct conflict with federal law, a decision made under a state constitution cannot be appealed to the Supreme Court.

At least twenty states guarantee the right of privacy through their constitutions or statutes. The Alaska Constitution, for example, declares: "The right of the people to privacy is recognized and shall not be infringed." California citizens are guaranteed "inalienable rights" in "pursuing and obtaining safety, happiness and privacy." The Montana Constitution decrees: "The right of individual privacy is essential to the well-being of a free society and shall not be infringed without the showing of compelling state interest."

Such constitutions may assume a pivotal role in the introduction of RU 486 into the United States. The power of the federal bureaucracy and the Bush administration to ban RU 486 research at the National Institutes of Health extends only to the use of federal funds. If a state decided to allot its own money to RU 486 development, the White House would have little chance of intervening.

At least twenty states have laws permitting their health departments to test and distribute any drugs that could be beneficial to their citizens. In New York, California and Connecticut, among others, such recent legislation could be classified as a "mini–FDA law." Connecticut, for example, allows the development of a drug "for investigational use." It must be made and distributed within the state so as not to conflict with the authority of the federal FDA. If Connecticut's health department, therefore, considered the development of a drug similar to RU 486 essential to public health (or RU 486 itself, depending on patent settlement), a highly qualified private company could begin production and trials.

Although these mini–FDA laws are too new to have been tested in court, they would probably stand up against a challenge from the Bush administration. Privacy may thus become the vehicle for a state to ensure that all procreative decisions rest with its citizens. Just as Connecticut has guaranteed through legislation the provisions of *Roe v. Wade*, it could also guarantee that a safe and efficient abortion pill becomes a similar, privacy-based right. This could be the long-awaited breakthrough, a breakthrough eventually providing American women with the same standard of medical treatment now enjoyed by women in Europe.

— 10 —
Bringing RU 486 into the United States

The pressures on the Roussel Company to release RU 486 into the American market have become acute in the nineties. Delegations have flown repeatedly to Paris to present arguments to Dr. Edouard Sakiz, the company president, on why RU 486 must be introduced quickly into the United States. Molly Yard, president of the National Organization for Women, and Dr. Allan Rosenfield, former chairman of the Planned Parenthood Federation, have lobbied Roussel on behalf of their delegations. Eleanor Smeal, president of the Fund for a Feminist Majority, brought petitions signed by 125,000 Americans urging immediate introduction of the pill. Dr. Étienne-Émile Baulieu, a leading developer of the pill, has insisted that the "key to the future of RU 486 lies in the United States," but none of these pressures has had any effect on Roussel.

Although a consultant to the company, Baulieu has attacked Roussel "for passing responsibility for international approval of the pill to the World Health Organization." According to the *New York Times,* Baulieu further charges that the WHO "has withheld approval out of anxiety that the United States may retaliate by cutting contributions to its budget."

WHO had a contract with Roussel for worldwide testing of RU 486 in recent years and could have initiated new tests at five or ten prominent American medical schools, which would have speeded up the admission process. Yet WHO apparently wanted to avoid a confrontation with the Bush administration. Referring to Hirochi Nagashima, director of WHO's Human Reproduction Unit, Baulieu complained, "The man says he's afraid that American money will be cut off if an RU 486 program comes under the WHO umbrella."

Roussel has remained convinced that RU 486 cannot be brought to the United States until the government requests an application from the company. Roussel's fears go far deeper than potential boycotts of Roussel products by anti-abortion groups and a political backlash from extremists. The company's greatest fear is a highly organized boycott by Catholic hospitals, which control approximately one-third of all hospital beds in the United States and represent 640 out of 3,289 nonprofit, nongovernmental institutions. If these Catholic hospitals refused as a bloc to buy any Hoechst-Roussel products, the company's sales could be severely reduced. While such a situation may be an unfortunate example of religious morality controlling medical practice, the implications of these statistics in business terms are all too clear.

Edward Norton, spokesman for Hoechst-Roussel Pharmaceuticals of New Jersey, denied the company's position in March 1990: "We've been petitioned, we've been yelled at, and we've been telephoned by everybody. But our formal position hasn't changed in two years, and I don't expect it to change." Arielle Moutet, head of international marketing for Roussel in Paris, announced in July 1990: "Selling in the United States is out of the question at the moment."

By 1990, many abortion rights organizations had decided that all such evidence proved RU 486 would not be introduced into the United States for perhaps as long as another decade unless some decisive action forced Roussel to change its position. Two threats make availability of the pill for American women more essential now than ever. With the resignation of Justice William Brennan from the Supreme Court and the seating of a conservative justice, David H. Souter, *Roe v. Wade* is in particular danger of being overthrown or at least weakened. Further, under the Court's recent *Webster* decision, some states, such as Pennsylvania, are already passing laws restricting access to abortion. It is a real possibility that the right to abortion could soon be limited to a handful of progressive states, and that most women would have to travel long distances at great expense to find an abortion clinic, posing an obvious hardship for the poor.

Only RU 486 can provide an alternative in case of a national erosion of abortion rights. If a state passes a restrictive law, an abortion clinic can be shut down, but it would be much harder to stop conscientious doctors from practicing what they consider good medicine and administering RU 486 in the privacy of their offices. The pill, therefore, must be introduced immediately not just to guarantee the health of women, but to convince legislatures and courts that women can never again be denied their fundamental rights.

Abortion rights groups have developed, over the past

several years, a set of plans by which RU 486 could finally be made available to American women. What follows is a description of several such strategies.

One plan was to have a doctor in London buy Roussel RU 486 pills, no matter what the cost, in France, Britain, or another European country. But abortion rights groups quickly learned that every pill released by Roussel to a hospital or clinic was numbered. Every pill had to be accounted for in official records, listing the name and address of each patient undergoing abortion. A doctor had to certify that the pill had been administered on the spot. This approach turned out to be fruitless.

Another plan was to buy pills from a country that had made a laboratory synthesis or exact copy of RU 486. The purpose would be to use these pills as a model against which scientists could check the structure and purity of the RU 486 pills that might be produced in the United States. In a lengthy exchange of letters, one group was able to convince an institution overseas how critically important the project could be for American women. The pills would be given to scientists coming to America to participate in international conferences, and the scientists could carry small quantities through U.S. customs in their personal possessions. Still, to ensure the safety of American women, the chemical structure of these pills would have to be verified by a chemist trained in steroids from a noted U.S. research center.

Dosage became an important issue in this plan. Although Dr. Jose Barzelatto of the Ford Foundation and Dr. Paul F. A. Van Look of the World Health Organization concluded that WHO tests worldwide had proved the safety and efficiency of a 200 milligram dose, the 600 milligram dose used in France had been so widely publicized that women would probably expect it had to be maintained. Any procedures done in the United States, therefore, would probably require three 200 milligram pills.

Another strategy was that a package of 200 milligram pills, mailed from a doctor overseas to an American doctor, could constitute a definitive test of the law today as a similar mailing had done for Margaret Sanger almost sixty years ago. The "One Package" case of 1936 involved a Japanese doctor who had mailed 120 rubber pessaries (a barrier device worn in the vagina) for contraceptive testing to Dr. Hannah Stone, medical director of Sanger's birth control clinic in New York. The U.S. government had seized them at customs, claiming their importation was forbidden by the Tariff Act. In a decision that vastly expanded the professional discretion of physicians, the U.S. Court of Appeals, Second Circuit, then the most prestigious appeals court in the country, ruled that the law could not prohibit the "importation of things which might be intelligently employed by conscientious and competent physicians to save life or promote well-being of patients." The "One Package" decision might be sweeping enough to cover importation of RU 486 pills today.

If U.S. Customs seized the pills, the receiving doctor could go into federal court, as Sanger had done, to force the government to return the package to him or her. Such a lawsuit could have important implications. A victory would give enough legitimacy to the abortion pill to rouse the indignation of American women and to put considerable pressure on the White House and the FDA.

The ultimate, final alternative would be to manufacture and test a copy of the pill in the United States and demonstrate to the White House and Congress the pill's importance to American women. This is a challenging concept, but to those who campaigned for abortion rights from 1966 on when almost no one else thought legal abortion would be feasible, testing and distributing RU 486 in this country is the only way to galvanize the public.

The legal strategy would depend upon at least a dozen new state laws. For example, a California statute, passed in 1988 and considered a mini–FDA law, allows "investigations" of a new drug to ensure it is "safe" and "effective." In his 1990 race for the Democratic nomination for governor of California, State Attorney General John K. Van de Kamp declared that this definition would allow increased testing in the state.

Consequently, a committee of leading doctors—the "RU 486 Medical Study Group," with offices at the State Medical Society—was formed to implement this approach. By late 1990, California not only had a governor, a legislature, and a medical society committed to abortion rights, but its state constitution included "privacy" among its "inalienable rights." Although the study group believed the Roussel Company would soon supply it with pills, other abortion rights leaders remained convinced this wouldn't happen for years, and that the essential step would be to manufacture the pill within the borders of a state having a mini–FDA law.

One strategy would be to go into a state such as New York or Connecticut where the state government is sympathetic to women's rights. Both states have mini–FDA laws similar to California's, and both have governors and legislatures committed to abortion rights. In fact, Connecticut recently passed a bill guaranteeing women all the protection of *Roe v. Wade* in case the Supreme Court overthrows or dilutes it.

These mini–FDA laws could allow the testing and distribution of a new drug provided that the drug was made within the state and distributed only in the state. To implement these laws, it would be necessary to persuade state authorities to exercise the powers they possess but have never used. It would be necessary to hire a research chemist, preferably one with experience working on RU 486 or similar steroids, to develop an exact copy in a laboratory within the state. All state medical standards would have to be scrupulously followed.

Another objective would be to secure the services of an obstetrician-gynecologist who would administer RU 486 and run the tests, preferably a highly skilled woman who would have the confidence of her patients and who had worked previously at abortion clinics. During the abortion procedure the doctor would be in constant touch with patients through visits and phone calls, and she would keep a detailed record of results for official analysis. A nearby hospital would be available in case of emergency. To guarantee that she had thorough knowledge of RU 486, the doctor would first go to France and Britain to study with doctors there who have long been involved in the administration of RU 486.

While in Europe, the doctor would also need to buy the prostaglandin that would have to be taken in conjunction with RU 486. The prostaglandin available in the United States is the wrong dose. Since the correct dosage is widely available in Britain and has long been used for midterm abortions, a European connection could guarantee an adequate supply.

One hurdle might remain in Paris. Since Roussel holds world patents on RU 486, it would be necessary to determine whether the company might challenge the manufacturing of a copy of the pill under state law. The case for manufacturing the pill in America would be put to Dr. Sakiz, the president of Roussel. The argument would be made that testing the pill in a number of states would absorb the initial political flak from the extremist opposition and pave the way for Roussel's eventual application for approval at the FDA. If the battle was won under state laws first, it would be a lot easier later for Roussel to gain approval from the FDA to sell the pill commercially in the United States.

Since the testing of RU 486 on women would be done on a nonprofit basis and patients would be treated free of charge, the testing would hardly be in conflict with a commercial license. The plan would call for testing to cease as soon as Roussel decided to enter the commercial market in America.

Making and testing the pill under state laws could be a unique and daring approach; no court precedents seem applicable to it. If the U.S. attorney general at the behest of the White House should decide to bring an injunction against testing, a critical court battle could ensue. The main principle at issue would be the scope of interstate commerce. The government might claim that any new drug came under federal authority, but since the pills were made and tested within a state whose law approved such testing, the interstate commerce power would probably be inapplicable.

Whatever action the government might bring, the bases of state laws should be sound enough to carry the case to the Supreme Court if necessary. With the health and rights of women at stake, any risks would seem worthwhile. No matter what the outcome, the battle would help to rally the country behind RU 486 and make its nationwide admission imperative.

The project to bring RU 486 into the United States must be a unified effort relying on many medical, civil rights, family planning, and women's groups. When all the pieces of the project are in place, the public will know at last whether RU 486 will become the "moral property" of women not just in France and other European countries, but in the United States as well.

Acknowledgments

It seems increasingly difficult with each book to express adequate appreciation to my wife, Joan Summers Lader. She not only has been a discerning critic of every chapter, but has offered her time unstintingly for the most detailed job of research, or fact-checking. Beyond this, she has contributed the love and stability necessary to keep a writer functioning. In addition, our daughter, Wendy Summers Lader, a law school student, made a substantial contribution to the legal analysis in this book.

My agent, Roberta Pryor, has continued to offer the wisdom and patience that have characterized her role for twenty-five years, and I cherish her as a friend and counselor.

My editors at Addison-Wesley, Martha Moutray and Jane Isay, have been invaluable critics and loyal organizers of the project from the start, ably assisted by Johanna Van Hise. Nancy Fish has put her consummate skills into public relations.

Dr. Jose Barzelatto of the Ford Foundation, a leading expert on RU 486, has graciously read the manuscript for medical and scientific accuracy. While he is in no way responsible for my opinions or errors, he has shared his knowledge and time in repreated interviews, and I am deeply indebted to him.

From the Alan Guttmacher Institute, Dr. Stanley Henshaw and Michael Klitsch have supplied documents, research, and guidance. Their unfailing help and friendship have contributed immensely to my work.

Marie Bass of the Reproductive Health Technologies Project has been a constant source of information and encouragement.

Steven Shapiro of the American Civil Liberties Union, and Edward N. Costikyan and Gail Heatherly of Paul, Weiss, Rifkind, Wharton & Garrison and Marshall Beil and Steven Delibert have supplied shrewd and essential legal analysis.

In Paris, and during his trips to Washington and New York, Dr. Étienne-Émile Baulieu has given me an exhaustive scientific and medical interpretation of RU 486 during many interviews, and his brilliance added immeasurably to the book. At the Roussel Company in Paris, executives and scientists who granted indispensable interviews include Dr. Edouard Sakiz, president, and Drs. Roger Deraedt, Daniel Philibert, Georges Teutsch, and André Ulmann.

In Paris, Dr. Elisabeth Aubeny of the Broussais Hospital, Drs. Danielle Gaudry and Sadan Ouri of the Mouvement Français pour le Planning Familial, Dr. Paul Robel of INSERM, Chautale Blayo of the Institut Nationale d'Étude Démographique, and Pontus Hulten were generous in supplying research documents and insights. Some of these doctors also provided access to interviews with RU 486 patients.

In Britain, I had the privilege of talking with the following experts: Drs. Timothy R. L. Black of Marie Stopes International, Ian Z. Mackenzie of Radcliffe Hospital in Oxford, and David Paintin of St. Mary's Hospital Medical School in London; and Dilys Cossey of the Family Planning Association, Dr. Pramilla Schanayake of the International Planned Parenthood Federation, and Madeleine Tearse of the Birth Control Trust.

By phone or by mail, Dr. Marc Bygdeman of the Karolinska Hospital in Stockholm, Dr. Paul F. A. Van Look of the World Health Organization in Geneva, and Anne-Marie Rey of the Swiss Union for De-criminalization of Abortion were unfailingly helpful in providing information and analysis.

In the United States, I profited from the knowledge I gained in interviews with many people among them: Drs. Amy Cousins, Peter Bours, and Curtis Boyd; Robin Duke and Ambassador Angier Biddle Duke; Drs. Carl Djerassi of Stanford University, David Grimes of the University of Southern Calfiornia, Richard Hausknecht, Gary D. Hodgen of East Virginia Medical School, Kathryn Horwitz of the University of Colorado, Seymour Lieberman of Columbia University, Sheldon Segal of the Rockefeller Foundation, Samuel Yen of the University of California School of Medicine at San Diego; and Nancy Larsen.

At the Population Council in New York, Drs. Wayne Bardin, James Phillips, Theodore Jackanicz, and Sandra Waldman contributed their expertise generously, as did Drs. George Chrousos and Lynette Nieman, and George Gaines of the National Institute of Health in Maryland.

Joan Dunlop and Drs. Sandra Kabir and Nahed Toubin of the International Women's Health Coalition, and Dr.

Atiquer Rahman Khan of the United Nations Fund for Population Activities gave me special insight into the family planning system of Bangladesh.

Many organizations concerned with RU 486 contributed substantially to my research. I want to thank in particular David Andrews, Douglas Gould, Barbara Snow, and Faye Wattleton of the Planned Parenthood Federation of America; Molly Yard and Marilyn Barnes of the National Organization for Women; Eleanor Smeal of the Fund for a Feminist Majority; Frances Kissling of Catholics for a Free Choice; Edith Tiger of the National Emergency Civil Liberties Committee; Kate Michelman and Dawn Johnson of the National Abortion Rights Action League; Steven Heilig of the RU 486 Medical Study Group; Diane Zuckerman of U.S. Representative Ted Weiss's staff; and Pat Richter of U.S. Representative Bill Green's staff.

Notes

INTRODUCTION

P.1   Commonwealth v. Bangs, 9 Mass. (Tyng) 387, 388 (1812); Commonwealth v. Parker, 50 Mass. (9 Met.) 263, 43 Am. Dec. 396 (1845).

p. 1   State v. Murphy, 27 N.J.L. 112 (Sup. Ct. 1858).

p. 2   Evans v. People, 49 N.Y. 86, 90 (1872).

p. 2   Mills v. Commonwealth, 13 Pa. 621 (1850).

p. 3   Lawrence Lader, *Abortion* (New York: Bobbs-Merrill Co., 1966), p. 8.

p. 4   Christopher Tietze, *National Institute of Mental Health Record* 16, no. 25 (16 Dec. 1964): 1; Harold Rosen, ed., *Abortion in America*, (Boston: Beacon Press 1967), paper.

p. 5   Sherri Finkbine: Judge Yale McFate opinion, Memo no. 140504, Superior Ct., State of Arizona, Cty. of Maricopa, July 31, 1962; Helen B. Taussig, "The Thalidomide Syndrome," *Scientific American*, Aug. 1962; *Arizona Republic*, July 23–Aug. 4, 1962.

p. 5–6   National Council: William H. Genné, "Abortion," *Concerns for Christian Citizens* 5, no. 4 (Jan. 1965): 1–2; Judaism: Solomon B. Freehof, *Recent Reform Responses* (Cincinnatti: Hebrew Union College Press, 1963).

p. 6   "Animated" soul: Roger J. Huser, *The Crime of Abortion in Common Law*, Canon Law Studies No. 162 (Washington, D.C.: Catholic University of America Press, 1942); John T. Noonan, Jr., *Contraception* (Cambridge, Mass.: Harvard University Press, 1965), 86, 232–3.

p. 6   Lader, *Abortion*, p. 173; Griswold v. Connecticut, 381 U.S. 479 (1965).

pp. 9–10   People v. Belous, 71 Cal.2d 954, 458 P.2d 194, 80 Cal. Rptr. 354 (1969), *cert. denied,* 397 U.S. 915 (1970); United States v. Vuitch, 305 F. Supp. 1032 (D.D.C. 1969), *jurisdiction postponed to asrguments on merits,* 397 U.S. 1061 (1970).

p. 11   Roe v. Wade, 410 U.S. 113 (1973).

p. 12   Law: Shannon, interview with author, 11 February 1986; New York Times, 24 March 1984, p. 1. Scheidler: Patricia Donovan, "The Holy War," *Family Planning Perspective,* Jan./Feb. 1985, 5–9.

p. 12   Lawrence Lader, *Abortion II,* (Boston: Beacon Press, 1973), p. ix.

CHAPTER ONE

P. 14   Evin: *Baltimore Sun,* 29 October 1988, p. 1A.

p. 14   Ian Mackenzie, interview with author, Oxford, England, 29 January 1990.

p. 15   "Bleeding similar to if slightly heavier": Louise Silvestre et al., "Voluntary Interruption of Pregnancy," *New England Journal of Medicine* 322, no. 10 (8 March 1990): 645; Marc Bygdeman et al., "Progesterone Receptor Blockage," *Contraception* 32, no. 1 (July 1985): 45.

p. 15   77 per cent French women: Elisabeth Aubeny, interview with author, Paris, 4 February 1990. 103 cases: Mackenzie, interview with author.

p. 16   Cyril C. Means, "The Laws of New York Concerning Abortion," *New York Law Forum* 14 (1968): 411–515; Means, "The Phoenix of Abortional Freedom," *New York Law Forum* 17 (1971): 335–410.

p. 17   "Death drug": *New York Times,* 28 October 1988, p. A34. "Human pesticide": *Christianity Today,* 9 December 1988, p. 16.

p. 18   Italy and Spain: Dr. Edouard Sakiz, interview with author, Paris, 1 February 1990.

p. 18   Russell Baker: *New York Times,* 9 June 1990, p. 23.

p. 18   Bombing, arson statistics: National Abortion Federation, Washington, D.C.

p. 19   Randall Terry: *New York Times,* 11 June 1990, p. A16.

p. 19   15 to 20 percent: Frances Kissling, telephone interview with author, 11 January 1990.

p. 20   Étienne-Émile Baulieu: Baulieu, "RU 486," *Journal of the American Medical Association* 262, no. 13 (6 Oct. 1989): 1808.

p. 21   David Grimes: *Detroit Free Press,* 22 Nov. 1988, p. B2; David Grimes, telephone interview with author, 16 July 1990.

p. 22   World Health Organization, botched abortions, "balance between man and nature": E. Diczfalusy et al., *Research in Human Reproduction* (WHO, Generva, 1988), 342, 500.

CHAPTER TWO

P. 24   *Science* quotation: *Science,* 22 Sept. 1988, p. 1319 *Nature:* 6 Oct. 1988, 48.

p. 24   Gregory Pincus, *The Control of Fertility,* (New York: Academic Press, 1965,) 114, 132.

p. 25   Seymour Lieberman, interview with author, New York, 23 November 1989.

p. 25   Étienne-Émile "I wanted my work": Baulieu, interview with author, Boston, 12 February 1990.

p. 25–26 Margaret Sanger, Russia, Worcester: Margaret Sanger, interview by author for biography, Tucson, Ariz., 1952.

p. 26   Russell Marker, Syntex Company: Carl Djerassi, *The Politics of Contraception,* (New York: W.W. Norton, 1979), p. 228.

p. 26   Norethindrone: Djerassi, *Politics of Contraception,* p. 248.

p. 27   RU 486 action, receptors, progesterone secretion: Klaus Lubke et al., "Hormonal receptors," *Angewandte Chemie International Edition in English* 15, no. 12, (1976): p. 741 Marc Bygdeman et al., "Progesterone Receptor Blockage," *Contraception,* 32:45, July 1985, No. 1 M.L. Swahn et al., "Effect of Antiprogestin RU 486," *British Journal of Obstetrics & Gynecology,* 95:126, 1988 Chander P. Puri, Paul F. A. Van Look, eds., *Hormone Antagonists for Fertility Regulation,* Symposium Proceedings, November 4, 1988, Bombay, India. Van Look chapter, "Hormonal Fertility Regulation," pp. 1–4, 11; H.B. Croxatto chapter, "Effects of RU 486 on the Menstrual Cycle," pp. 141–51 Interviews with Baulieu at INSERM, Teutsch, Philibert, other scientists at Roussel Company, Paris, 31 January–2 February 1990.

p. 27   Paul Ehrlich, *Ber. Dtsch. Chem. Ges.,* 42:17, 1909. Elwood V. Jensen, *Proceedings of the National Academy of Sciences,* 15 February 1968, v. 592, p. 632.

p. 28   Bert O'Malley, "Recent Progress in Hormone Research," v.

25, (New York: Academic Press, 1969) pg. 105. O'Malley, "Hormonal Control" in R.O. Greep et al., *Frontiers in Reproduction*, (Cambridge, Mass.: M.I.T. Press, 1977) p. 236.

p. 28   "No one knew," "You don't know": Baulieu, interviews with author, Paris, 31 January–3 February 1990.

p. 28   "Binding system responds": Edwin Milgrom et al., "Progesterone in Uterus and Plasma," *Steroids*, December 1970, v. 16, no. 6, p. 741

p. 29   "Chemistry is like building": Teutsch interview with author, 1 February 1990

p. 29   "Potent synthetic progestin": Daniel Philibert, J. P. Raynaud, "Binding of Progestin and R 5020," *Contraception*, November 1974, v. 10, p. 457.

p. 29   R 2323: Edouard Sakiz et al., "A New Approach to Estrogen-Free Contraception," *Contraception*, November 1974, v. 10, no. 3, p. 467.

p. 29   "Receptor concentration": Baulieu, "Steroid Receptors and Hormone Receptivity," *Journal of the American Medical Association* 27 October 1975, v. 234, no. 4, p. 104.

p. 30   "Progesterone-induced changes": Genevieve Azadian-Boulanger et al., *American Journal of Obstetrics & Gynecology*, 15 August 1976, v. 125, Part 2, p. 1049.

p. 30   "Highest-binding qualities": Teutsch, interview with author, Pans, February 1990.

p. 30   "Shotgun approach": Interview N.I.H., 13 December 1989. Teutsch, Philibert letter: private correspondence with author.

p. 30   Eleven pregnant women: Walter Herrmann et al., "Effect of an Antiprogesterone Steroid," *Comptes Rendus de l'Académie des Sciences*, 294: 933, 1982.

p. 31   100 women: B. Couzinet et al., "Termination of Early Pregnancy," *New England Journal of Medicine*, 18 December 1986, v. 315, no. 25, p. 1565.

p. 31   340 women: E. Aubeny et al., "Clinical Study of 353 Cases," *Contraception, Fertilité, Sexualité*, 1989, v. 17, no. 4, p. 307.

p. 31–32 WHO test sites: D. Shoupe et al., "Progesterone Termination," *Contraception*, May 1986, v. 33, no. 5, p. 455.

p. 32   "Combined therapy": Bygdeman, "Progesterone Receptor," op. cit.; Catherine Dubois et al., "Contragestion by RU 486," *C.R. Acad Sci Paris*, T 306, Series III, 1988, pp. 57–61.

p. 32   Success rate of RU 486: Louise Silvestre et al., "Voluntary Interruption of Pregnancy," *New England Journal of Medicine*, 8 March 1990, v. 322, no. 10, p. 645. Success rate has been corroborated in 10,615 cases reported in unpublished paper by André Ulmann of Roussel Company to symposium at Tbilisi, U.S.S.R., 10–13 October 1990.

p. 32–33   Prostaglandin patent: Sakiz, interview with author, Paris, 2 February 1990.

p. 33   "Body for several days": Interviews, Jose Barzelatto 6 December 1989, Mike Klitsch 12 March 1990.

p. 33   "Risk for the conceptus": Baulieu, "RU 486 as an Antiprogresterone Steroid," *Journal of the American Medical Association.* 6 October 1989, v. 262, no. 13, pp. 1808–14, particularly FN 44.

p. 33   Roger Henrion: *Nature,* 9 March 1989, p. 110

CHAPTER THREE

P. 35   "Introduced Sakiz to the company," "You are successful": Author interviews with Roussel scientists, 1–2 February 1990.

p. 37   Baulieu's "extraordinary intelligence": Lieberman, interview with author, 23 November 1989 "Very original scientists,": Chrousos, interview with author, N.I.H., Bethesda, Maryland, 13 December 1989. Jean Bernard: "L'Épée D'Académicien Du Professeur Étienne Baulieu" (pamphlet), 26 October 1983, Paris, pp. 25, 47, 49.

p. 37   "Most controversial scientist": Earle Holland, Columbus, Ohio, *Dispatch,* 8 October 1989 (column).

p. 37   "Baulieu could get an appointment": Sakiz, interview with author, Paris, 2 February 1990.

p. 37   Home of Walter Annenberg: Interview with author–subject requested anonymity.

p. 38   "Political Animal": Horwitz, interview by phone with author, 15 March 1990.

p. 38   "One-man show" and par. following: Interview with author–subject requested anonymity; Sakiz, Ulmann, Duke, interviews with author, 2 February, 5 February, and 9 January 1990.

p. 38   Baulieu "highest ski exam" and "obsession": Baulieu, interview with author, Paris, 5 February 1990.

p. 38 Lieberman, interview with author, New York City, 23 November 1989.

p. 38 "Collect postcards": Baulieu, interview with author, New York, 9 February 1990.

p. 38 Robin Duke: Interview with author, New York, 9 January 1990.

p. 39 Sophia Loren: Interview with author—subjects requested anonymity, Paris, 5 February 1990.

p. 39 Robel, Bernard, "L'Épée D'Académicie" op. cit., pp. 39, 49.

p. 39 "Leave dinner party": Baulieu, interview with author, New York, 9 February 1990.

p. 39–40 Baulieu information on family, mother, gym classes, Nazis, Communist party: Baulieu, interviews with author, Paris, 31 January 1990.

p. 40 U.S. visa: Lieberman, interview with author, 23 November 1989.

p. 40–41 "Angry in those days": Pontus Hulten, interview with author, Paris, 5 February 1990.

p. 41 "Doing molecular biology": Baulieu, interview with author, Paris, 2 February 1990.

p. 41 AIDS virus: *New York Times*, 24 March 1990, p. A6.

p. 41 "Synthesized in April 1980": Joseph Palca, "The Pill of Choice?" *Science*, 22 September 1989, v. 245 pp. 1319–57; Teutsch letter, v. 247, p. 622

p. 42 "Responsible for receptor screening": Teutsch, interview with author, Paris, 1 February 1990.

p. 42 "Influence on Sakiz": Daraedt, interview with author, Paris, 1 February 1990.

p. 42 "His pressure on top management": Baulieu, interview with author, Paris, 31 January 1990. Roussel Uclaf Release, SCRIP, no. 1473, 15 December 1989.

p. 42–43 "Worked hard at mediation" and whole para: Sakiz, Baulieu, interviews with author, Paris, 2 February 1990.

p. 44 Catholic church reactions: Interviews with U.S. reporters, Paris, 5 February 1990.

p. 44 Catholic doctors letters: Private correspondence, in author's files.

p. 44 Geslin: *New York Times*, 27 October 1988, p. A1

p. 44 Independence from Hoechst and retreat: Sakiz, interview with author, Paris, 2 February 1990.

p. 44 Rio de Janeiro meeting: Allan Rosenfield, interview with author, New York, 9 November 1989.

p. 44 Dr. Bureau: *New York Times*, 27 October 1988, p. A1. "Morally scandalous": U.S. reporter, interview with author, Paris, 5 February 1990.

p. 45 "Last Temptation of Christ": U.S. reporter, interview with author, Paris, 5 February 1990; *New York Times*, 24 October 1988, p. A3; October 25, p. C21; November 9, p A6.

p. 45 Evin: Health Minister letter to author; *New York Times*, 29 October 1988. p. A1; Roussel Uclaf SCRIP, no. 1358, 4 November 1988.

p. 45 Catholic opposition dwindled: Elisabeth Aubeny, interview with author, Paris, 4 February 1990.

CHAPTER FOUR

P. 46 Women's reactions in first two pars.: Social workers' notes from Broussais Hospital; *Médecine et Hygiène* report of 11 August 1988, in *WGNR Newsletter 31*, October–December 1989, p. 7; *Le Nouvel Observateur/Norte Époque*, 30 March 1988, p. 130; *Philadelphia Inquirer*, 30 July 1989, p. 1A; *Miami Herald*, 1 April 1989; Elisabeth Aubeny, interview with author, Paris, 4 February 1990.

p. 46–47 Kyle X: telephone interview requesting anonymity

p. 47 "A thousand RU 486 cases": Aubeny, interview with author, Paris, 4 February 1990 and report, pp. 4–6.

p. 47 "A third of French women": Sheldon Segal note, (p. 691), *New England Journal of Medicine*, 8 March 1990, v. 322, no. 10.

p. 47 "De-medicalized abortion," "grow up,": Birman, *WGNR Newsletter*, op. cit. pp. 8–9.

p. 48 "Everything done quickly" and whole par.: Aubeny, interview with author, Paris, 4 February 1990.

p. 49 French abortion statistics: Chautale Blayo, interview by phone with author, Paris, 5 February 1990; Institut National d'Étude Démographique

p. 49 Pregnancy statistics among unmarried girls: Stanley Henshaw, interview with author, New York City, 26 March 1990

p. 49–50 RU 486 complications: Aubeny, interview with author, Paris, 4 February 1990.

p. 50   "No pain at all": Aubeny, interview with author, Paris, 4 February 1990.

p. 50   WHO study: Paul F.A. Van Look et al., "Termination of Early Human Pregnancy with RU 486," *Human Reproduction*, v. 4, no. 6, 1989, p. 718.

p. 50   Radcliffe Hospital statistics: Ian Z. Mackenzie interview with author, Oxford, 29 January 1990.

p. 50   "Two different types of prostaglandin": Louise Silvestre et al, "Voluntary Interruption of Pregnancy," *New England Journal of Medicine*, 8 March 1990, v. 322, no. 10, p. 645.

p. 50–51   "Some women may drop out": Danielle Gaudry, Sadan Ouri, interview with author, Paris, 2 February 1990.

p. 51   Bureau: *WGNR Newsletter*, op. cit. p. 9.

p. 51   British trials: Mackenzie, interview with author, Oxford, 29 January 1990.

p. 51–52   French system for RU 486: "Practical Guidelines, RU486" (pamphlet), (Paris: Mouvement Français pour le Planning Familial, 1989) pp. 3–4.

p. 51   Expulsion: Van Look, *Human reproduction*, op. cit.

p. 52–53   "Dedicated proponents of the Mouvement Français" and following par.": Gaudry, Ouri interview with author, 2 February 1990; "Practical Guidelines," op cit. p. 12.

p. 53   British Birth Control Trust, poll and following par.: Dilys Cossey, David Paintin, interviews with author, London, 26 and 29 January 1990.

p. 53   Marie Stopes International: Timothy R.L. Black, interview with author, London, 26 January 1990.

p. 54   British approval process: Cossey, Paintin, interview with author, 26 and 29 January 1990.

p. 54   "Monetary advantage": Mackenzie interview with author, Oxford, 29 January 1990.

p. 54   "Pressure on the government": Interviews with Cossey, Paintin, op. cit.

p. 55   British mid-term abortions and RU486: Mark Selinger et al., "Progesterone Inhibition in Mid-trimester Termination," *British Journal of Obstetrics & Gynecology*, December 1987, v. 94, p. 1218, *British Journal of Obstetrics & Gynecology*, December 1989, v. 96, p. 1424.

p. 55   Chinese trials on 2,000 women: Letter from Gao-Ji of Chinese National Research Institute for Family Planning to author; Gao-Ji et al., "Pregnancy Interruption with RU 486,"

Contraception, December 1988, v. 38, no. 6, p. 675; Shi Yong-en et al., "A Pharmacokinetic Study of RU486 and Its Metabolites," Shanghai Institute of Planned Parenthood Research (manuscript).

p. 56   Swedish "medical abortion at home" and following two pars: A.-S. Rosen et al, "Randomized Comparison of Prostaglandin Treatment," *Contraception*, May 1984, v. 29, no. 5, p. 423.

CHAPTER FIVE

P. 57–58   "Hemorrhage has been almost negligible": Silvestre, "Voluntary Interruption," *New England Journal of Medicine*, 8 March 1990, v. 322, no. 10, p. 645; unpublished reports from Aubeny, Mackenzie.

p. 58   World population: United Nations Fund for Population Activities, 1989 report, p. 56.

p. 58   Bangladesh unemployment: International Women's Health Coalition, "Population Control & Women's Health" (pamphlet), June 1988, New York, p. 2.

p. 59   "Untrained quacks": Letter from Dr. Abdua Choudjuri in Alan Guttmacher Institute files.

p. 59   Zarina: "Population Control," op. cit. p. 3.

p. 59–60   Family Welfare Visitors, Menstrual Regulation: Syeda Firoza Begum et al., "A Study on Menstrual Regulation Providers in Bangladesh," Bangladesh Association for Prevention of Septic Abortion (BAPSA), Dhaka (no date); "Evaluation of Menstrual Regulation Services in Bangladesh," BAPSA, 1987; Syeda F. Begum, "Menstrual Regulation Services & Training Program," BAPSA, 1985; letter of 30 June 1988 to Stanley Henshaw, from Bangladesh Fertility Research Institute; *Menstrual Regulation Newsletter*, Dhaka, December 1987, p. 3; September 1988, p. 1

p. 60   Bangladesh Women's Health Coalition: This par. and all pars. on Menstrual Regulation from interviews with James Phillips, 31 May 1990; Nahed Toubin of Population Council; Joan Dunlop; Sandra Kabir of International Women's Health Coalition, 4 June 1990.

p. 61   "Complications after receiving MR services": R. Amin et al., "Menstrual Regulation in Bangladesh," *International Journal of Obstetrics & Gynecology*, 27: 1988, pp. 265–271.

p. 61   "Westernizing" Bangladesh women: Atiquer Rahman Khan interview with author, New York City, 31 May 1990

p. 62–63   WHO trials and RU 486 low dosage, this and two following pars.: Jose Barzelatto and Paul F.A. Van Look interviews with author, by telephone, 12 June 1990 and 13 June 1990.

p. 63   "Combining RU 486 and prostaglandin" and following par.: Barzelatto, Sakiz, interviews with author, 12 June and 2 February 1990.

p. 64   "Introduction of RU 486 into Britain": Dilys Cossey, David Paintin, Madeleine Tearse, interviews with author, London, 26 and 29 January 1990.

p. 64–66   German unification and abortion and following three pars.: *New York Times,* July 19, 1990, pl A1: July 23, p. A3: Alan Guttmacher Institute files.

p. 66–67   "Abortion politics of Poland" and following three pars.: Malgorzata Dobraczynska and Barbara Limanowksa of Polish Feminist Association, memos of 20 May 1990, Klub Kobiet Korte, Amsterdam; *New York Times,* 29 May 1989, p. A1.

p. 67   "National-Catholic conservatives": Press conference memo of 28 May 1990, Berne, Switzerland; Hanna Jankowska, Polish Feminist Association; Iris Rossing, East-West Group.

p. 67   "Terrible irony of history": Anne-Marie Rey, telephone interview with author, on Polish abortion, Switzerland, 25 July 1990.

CHAPTER SIX

P. 70   "Contraceptive research has been held back": Hodgen, National Institutes of Health memo, "Summary of RU 486 Research Projects Involving RU 486," 28 March 1986, p. 7, 8.

p. 70   Lynette Nieman, "Progesterone Antagonist RU 486," *New England Journal of Medicine,* 22 January 1987, v. 316, p. 187. Paul F.A. Van Look et al., "Antiprogestational Steroids" in S.R. Milligan, ed. *Oxford Review of Reproductive Biology,* v. 2, (Oxford and New York: Oxford University Press,) 1989, p. 29; Nieman interview with author, Bethesda, Maryland, 13 December 1989.

p. 70–71   Danforth study, "blocks ovulation": Douglas R. Danforth, "Contraceptive Potential of RU 486", *Contraception*, August 1989, v. 40, no. 2, p. 195; T. Luukinem et al., "Inhibition of Folliculogenesis," *Fertility & Sterility*, 49 (B): 1988, p. 961; Jan F.H.M. Van Uem et al., "RU 486," *Contraception*, August 1989, v. 40, no. 2, p. 171.

p. 71   "Combination with a prostaglandin analogue": Van Look in Milligan, op cit., p. 31.

p. 71   "Although this research": Tina Agoestina, "Prospective Usefulness of RU 486," *Contraception*, Supp. to v. 36, 1987, p. 33.

p. 71   "Most optimistic results": Interview with Samuel Yen by telephone 25 April 1990 and with Jose Barzelatto, New York, 19 March 1990, and Étienne Baulieu, Boston, 12 February 1990.

p. 72   "Taken around 24 hours after ovulation": *Chicago Tribune*, 3 October 1989, p. 5: and private correspondence from Bygdeman to author, 29 March 1990.

p. 72   Hodgen, "opening the cervix": *New York Times*, 22 February 1988, p. 1. Garfield, "success rate": R. E. Garfield, "Effects of Antiprogesterone Compounds," in Chander P. Puri, Paul F.A. Van Look, eds., "Hormone Antagonists for Fertility Regulation," Symposium Proceedings, 4 November 1988, Bombay, India, p. 81.

p. 72–73   "Abnormal fetuses": N.I.H. memo, op. cit., p. 5; see also "Induction of Labor," *Lancet*, 1985 2 (8642): 1019; "Use of RU 486 for Cervical Dilatation," in Puri, Van Look, op. cit., p. 163.

p. 73   Cushing's Syndrome: N.I.H. memo, op. cit., p. 10; George Chrousos, interview with author, Bethesda, Maryland, 13 December 1989.

p. 74   Brain tumors: Interviews with Daniel Philibert, Paris, 1 February 1990 and Steven Grunberg by telephone, 3 May 1990.

p. 74   Endometriosis, endometrial cancer: N.I.H. memo, op. cit., pp. 8, 12.

p. 75   Ovarian, breast cancer: N.I.H. memo, ibid, p. 12

p. 76   "Stop at a woman's skin": adaptation of a phrase used by Gloria Steinem at Abortion Rights Mobilization dinner, 13 February 1989.

CHAPTER SEVEN

P. 77   *New York Times*/CBS poll: *New York Times*, 29 September
           1989, p. A13.

p. 77–78   Pope John Paul II: *New York Times*, 15 May 1985, p. A10;
           May 11, 1990, p. A10.

p. 78   Catholics, 30 per cent higher: S.K. Henshaw et al., "Char-
           acteristics of Prior Contraceptive Use," *Family Planning Per-
           spectives*, v. 20, July/August 1988, p. 158.

p. 79   Catholic publication of favored candidates: *Today's Catho-
           lic,* San Antonio, Tex., 2 May 1980; *St. Cloud Visitor,* Minn.,
           2 September 1982; *Jackson Citizen Patriot,* Mich., 10 Janu-
           ary 1986; *Our Lady of Good Counsel Parish Bulletin,* Vienna,
           Va., September 1982.

p. 79   Abortion Rights Mobilization lawsuit: *In re* United States
           Catholic Conference, 885 F. 2d 1020 (2d Cir. 1989), *cert.
           denied,* No. 89-1242 (April 30, 1990).

p. 79   San Diego election: *New York Times*, 11 November 1989,
           p. A18.

p. 80   Guam abortion legislation: *New York Times*, 21 March 1990,
           p. A24.

p. 80   Cardinal O'Connor on Gov. Cuomo: *New York Times*, 24
           January 1990, p. B1; 1 February 1990, p. A1.

p. 80   U.S. Senators Leahy, DeConcini: *New York Times*, 25 June
           1990, p. A1.

p. 81   French demonstrations "dwindled away," Spain, Italy:
           Steven Greenhouse, interview with author, Paris, 5 Feb-
           ruary 1990.

p. 82   Louisiana anti-abortion bill: *New York Times*, 24 June 1990,
           p. A23.

p. 82   Judie Brown: *New York Times*, 16 March 1990, p. A35;
           "Validity of," 11 November 1983, p. A27; Jim West, ACLU
           Reproductive Rights, 16 February 1990 p. 8.

p. 83   Adolescent Family Life Act: P.L. 97-35 300Z (b) (1) & (2).
           Jepsen: *Congressional Record*, S 6324, June 17, 1981.

p. 83   Gallup poll: Gallup, interview with author by phone 30
           May 1990.

p. 83   Scheidler, "disgusting": *Church & State*, April 1985, p. 18,
           quoting Jeffrey Hart column."
           "Opposed to all methods": *Dallas Morning News*, 1 October
           1989, p. A1.

p. 83   Robert Marshall: *Dallas Morning News,* ibid. Douglas Johnson: *New York Times,* 15 February 1990, p. A1; *Tampa Tribune & Times,* 19 March 1989

p. 84   Three million "annually at risk": Elise P. Jones et al., "Contraceptive Failure in the United States," *Family Planning Perspectives,* v. 21, May/June 1989, p. 103.

p. 84   "Twenty-eight per cent of all households": Tom, Nancy Biracree, eds. *Almanac of the American People,* (N.Y.-Oxford: Facts on File, 1988,) p. 71.

p. 85   "Excommunication Now," "Perverts on Parade": *New York Times,* 25 June 1990, p. B4.

p. 85   Bishop Vath: *New York Times,* 20 January 1985, p. A24. "In 1990 in the New York area": ACLU *Reproductive Rights,* 16 March 1990, p. 5.

p. 85   *New York Times,*-CBS poll, op cit.

p. 86   Minnesota case: *Hodgson v. Minnesota* No. 89-1125 upholding 8th circ. U.S. Ct. Ap. in St. Paul; see also *Ohio v. Akron Center for Reproductive Health* No. 88-805 reversing 6th circ. U.S. Ct. Ap. in Cincinnatti.

p. 86   Dearie, Spano: *Pro Choice* newsletter, Westchester Coalition for Legal Abortion, Mamaroneck, N.Y., June 1990, p. 1.

p. 86–87   Eagleton Institute poll: *Newark Star Ledger,* 9 April 1989, p. A1; Frances Avallone interview with author by telephone 31 May 1990

p. 87   Bristol, Conn., Rhode Island, Massachusetts: Lader, *Politics, Power and the Church,* (New York: Macmillan Publishing Co., 1987,) p. 227.

p. 87   Connecticut abortion rights bill: *New York Times,* 28 April 1990, p. A1.

p. 88   Lee Atwater: *New York Times,* 20 January 1990, p. A10.

CHAPTER EIGHT

P. 90   "Our scientists are under": George Gaines, interview with author, Bethesda, Maryland, 13 December 1989.

p. 90   "Social Civil War": *Tampa Tribune & Times,* 19 March 1989, p. A1.

p. 90   "The easy way to do this study": "Summary of NIH Research Projects Involving RU 486," March 1986, p. 7.

p. 90–91   Parkinson's: Parkinson's Disease Foundation, interview with author, by phone; ACLU *Reproductive Rights,* 16 February

1990, p. 2. Arlen Adams, Birt Harvey: *New York Times,* 2 November 1989, p. A1.

p. 91   AID, Foreign Operations bill: ACLU *Reproductive Rights,* 24 November 1989, p. 3.

p. 91–92   United Nations Population Conference: interviews with Paul Micou, David Poindexter, Steve Viederman. March 1986. For White House amendment to Document E/Conf. 76/5: Deirdre Wulf et al, "Consensus and Controversaries," *International Family Planning Perspectives,* September 1984, p. 81. For Clausen: *Population Today,* Population Reference Bureau, October 1984, p. 8.

p. 92   Boycott of Planned Parenthood: "The Priests of Berks County Want You to Know," *Newsletters* No. 1, mailed to St. Peter's Church, St. Margaret's Church, Reading, Pa. Reading *Times,* Reading *Eagle,* 18, 21 March, 1981.

p. 92   Louis Harris poll: "Attitudes About TV, Sex and Contraceptive Advertising," New York: Planned Parenthood Federation of America, February 1987

p. 93   Boycott of Upjohn: *New York Times,* 22 February 1988, Sec. I, p. 12. McDonough: Letter of April 19, 1989 to Sharon Camp of Population Crisis Committee.

p. 93   Cytotec boycott: *New York Times,* 28 October 1988, p. A34. Greener: *Chicago Sun-Times,* 25 December 1989.

p. 94   Rev. Dupin: *Richmond News Leader,* 3 November 1988, p. A15.

p. 94   Italy, Spain "more stable markets": Edouard Sakiz, interview with author, Paris, 2 February 1990.

p. 95   NIH budget, Djerassi: Carl Djerassi, "The Bitter Pill," *Science,* 28 July 1989, v. 245, p. 356.

p. 95   National Academy Report: Luigi Mastroianni, "Development of Contraception," *New England Journal Medicine,* 1990 482:4, p. 322.

p. 95–96   Norplant: Sandra Waldman, interview with author, New York City, 12 September 1990.

p. 96   Dalkon Shield: Sybil Shainwald, interview with author, New York City 12 September 1990.

p. 96–97   Drug company lawsuits: Nancy Larsen, interview with author, New York City 28 March 1990.

p. 97   Louis Harris poll, RU 486: May 1988 for Planned Parenthood, in Communications Consortium memo, 7 December 1989.

p. 98   Editorial, *Boston Globe*, 14 February 1990.

p. 98   Editorial, *Washington Post*, 17 February 1990.

p. 98   Editorial, *New York Times*, March 25, 1988, p. A38.

p. 98   American Bar Association: *New York Times*, 9 August 1990, p. A20.

p. 98–99 California Medical Association: Resolution 702-90, March 3–7, 1990; *New York Times*, 29 June 1990, p. A16.

p. 99   FDA "unapproved products": Rebecca Cook, "Antiprogestin Drugs," *Family Planning Perspectives*, v. 21, November/December 1989, p. 267.

p. 99   House Government Operations, U.S. Rep. Waxman: Diane Zuckerman interview by telephone with author, 20 July 1990; *New York Times*, 10 September 1990, p. A18.

p. 100   American College of Obstetrics & Gynecology poll: *Newsday*, 8 November 1989, II, p. 4.

p. 100   "Abortion would be as private": *New York Times*, 10 January 1990, p. A26.

p. 100–101 Eduardo Aquino and following two paras.: Aquino, "Right to Lifers Nearly Destroyed My Family," *Medical Economics*, 6 November 1989, p. 48 (Copyright 1989, Medical Economics, Inc. Reprinted by permission of *Medical Economics*.).

p. 101-102 Curtis Boyd and following par.: Testimony, U.S. House subcommittee on civil and constitutional rights, March 15, 1990; Boyd, interview with author by telephone, 20 March 1990.

p. 102   Peter Bours, Interview with author by telephone 20 March 1990

p. 103–104 Amy Cousins and following five pars.: Interview with author, New York 21 May 1990; *Newsday*, 8 November 1989, II, p. 4.

p. 104   New York clinics: *Terry v. New York NOW*, No. 89-1408, cert. denied 58 U.S.L.W. 3735 (May 21, 1990)

p. 105   "Only 27,000 abortions were done": Stanley Henshaw et al., "Abortion Services in the United States," *Family Planning Perspectives*, v. 22, May/June 1990, p. 102.

p. 107   "Most comprehensive of rights": *Olmstead v. U.S.*, 277 U.S. 438 (1928).

p. 107   Louis Harris poll: Alan F. Westin, *The Dimensions of Privacy*, (New York: Garland Publishing Co., 1981,) p. 5.

p. 107–108 "Privacy of women's bodies" and following two pars.: Veronika E.B. Kolder et al., "Court Ordered Obstetrical Interventions," *New England Journal Medicine*, v. 316, 7 May 1987, pp. 1192–1196; *New York Times*, 23 November 1987, p. A1; 23 March 1988, p. A17.

p. 108   *Griswold v. Connecticut*, 381 U.S. 479 (1965)

p. 108   *Roe v. Wade*, 410 U.S. 113 (1973)

p. 108   William Blackstone, "The Law of Criminal Abortion," *Indiana Law Journal*, v. 32, (1956–57), pp. 193–194.

p. 109   Early U.S. laws on abortion: Eugene Quay, "Justifiable Abortion—Medical and Legal Foundations," *Georgetown Law Journal*, v. 49, no. 3 (spring 1961), pp. 395–526; Cyril C. Means, "The Laws of New York Concerning Abortion," *New York Law Forum*, 14: 411–515, 1968.

p. 109   "Philosophic ramifications of privacy": Louis Brandeis, Samuel Warren, "The Right to Privacy," *Harvard Law Review*, v. 4, no. 5, December 1890, p. 193.

p. 109   *Boyd v. United States*, 116 U.S. 616 (1886).

p. 109   *Union Pacific Railway Company v. Botsford*, 141 U.S. 250 (1891).

p. 110   "To view pornography at home": *Stanley v. Georgia*, 349 U.S. 557 (1969).

p. 110   Georgia case, "power to control their bodies": *Bowers v. Hardwick*, 478 U.S. 186 (1986).

p. 110   Douglas, Goldberg: *Griswold*, op cit.

p. 111   "Right of privacy means anything": *Eisenstadt v. Baird*, 405 U.S. 438 (1972).

p. 111   Blackmun: *Roe v. Wade*, op. cit.

p. 111   Blackmun, "So foments disregard": *Webster v. Reproductive Health Services*, (1989 U.S.) 106 L Ed 2d 410, 109 S. Ct. 3040

p. 112   Rehnquist, *Reproductive*, op. cit.

p. 112   Supreme Court, "clear and convincing": *New York Times*, 26 June 1990, p. A1. *In Re Quinlan*, 355 A 2d 647 N.J. Sup. Ct. (1976) *Gruzan v. Missouri Department of Health*, 58 U.S.L.W. 4916 (1990).

p. 112   Larry McAfee: Ga. Code, Ann. Sec. 26-3003; *New York Times*, 22 November 1989, p. A18.

p. 113   Florida State Supreme Court: *New York Times*, 6 October 1989, p. A15.

p. 113   Alaska constitution, privacy: Art. I, Sec. 5.

p. 113   California constitution, privacy: Art. I, Sec. 1.

p. 113   Montana constitution, privacy: Art. II, Sec. 10.

p. 114   Connecticut "mini-FDA law": General Statutes of Connecticut, Title 21A, Consumer Protection, Chapter 418, Uniform Food, Drug and Cosmetic Act, Conn. Gen. Stat. 21a-110 (formerly Sec. 19-229).

p. 114   California "mini-FDA law": California Health & Safety Code 26021, 26670.

p. 115–116   Baulieu quotes: *New York Times*, 29 July 1990, p. A1.

p. 116   Catholic hospitals: "Statistical Abstracts of the U.S.," U.S. Department of Commerce, Bureau of Census, Washington, D.C., 1990.

p. 116   Norton: *Los Angeles Times*, 9 March 1990, p. A27.

p. 116   Moutet: *New York Times*, 29 July 1990, p. A1.

p. 118   Barzelatto, interview with author, New York City, 12 June 1990; Van Look, interview with author by phone, Geneva, 13 June 1990.

p. 118   "One Package": 86 F (2d) 737 Dec. 7, 1936.

p. 120   New York Education Law, Title VIII, The Professions, Article 137, Pharmacy NY CLS Educ 2 6817: New Drugs: General Statutes of Connecticut, Title 21 A, Consumer Portection, Chapter 418 Uniform Food, Drug & Cosmetic Act, Sec. 21 a-110, New Drugs.

Index

THE AUTHOR

Lawrence Lader has long been recognized as the pioneering writer on abortion rights and family planning in the country. His biography of Margaret Sanger was published in 1955. His book *Abortion* in 1966—the first to advocate a woman's total control over her reproductive life—opened a national debate on one of the most controversial issues of our time and was cited often in *Roe v. Wade*, the U.S. Supreme Court decision legalizing abortion. Lader was presented with the National Organization for Women's Certificate of Distinction for "Outstanding Leadership for Women's Rights" in April, 1989.

As founding chair of National Abortion Rights Action League (1969–1975), Lader helped put together the campaign producing the landmark New York state law of 1970. Since 1975 he has been president of Abortion Rights Mobilization.

A former adjunct associate professor in New York University's school of journalism and former president of American Society of Authors and Journalists, Lader has written more than 450 articles for *American Heritage, Collier's, New York Times Magazine, New Republic* and other national magazines. He is married to Joan Summers, a former opera singer.